"Thoroughly biblical in its scope and treatm
gifted the people of God with a manifesto t
part of what God is doing in cities. Incredib
and convincingly prophetic, this is a book y
and over again."

    Bryan Loritts, Lead Pastor, Fellowship Memphis; author, *A Cross Shaped Gospel*

"Jon Dennis provides a pastorally sound and culturally engaged response to questions the church is now asking in the face of rapid global urbanization. More commendably, he answers these questions with an eye toward the application of the gospel to the heart of the 'urban generation.' No matter their geographic location—city or suburb, high-rise or homestead—*Christ + City* will serve those hoping to broaden their perspective while deepening their commitment to the gospel."

    Stephen T. Um, Senior Minister, Citylife Presbyterian Church, Boston; author, *Why Cities Matter*

"Jon's book will equip Christian urbanites to reach cities for the gospel. He covers a broad spectrum of topics ranging from ambition and sex to ethnicity and children with twenty-first-century relevance and biblical insight. My prayer is that this book will lead to gospel clarity, encourage gospel living, fuel gospel prayers, and fire up gospel proclamation across the world from Chicago to Christchurch."

    Denesh Divyanathan, Founding Pastor, The Crossing Church, Singapore; President, Project Timothy

"Jon Dennis is a pastor, mentor, and visionary leader who has embraced Christ's call to the city. His dynamic ministry in Chicago and his outreach to other global cities across several continents give him a deep understanding of the opportunity that today's urban generation has to reach the city for Christ. In this pervasively gospel-centered book, Dennis combines the faithful exposition of central biblical texts with wise pastoral guidance to help people who live, work, serve, and worship in urban communities to honor God's redemptive purposes for the city."

    Philip Ryken, President, Wheaton College

"Is our view of the city simplistic? Is it overly positive, overly negative? Will our proclamation of King Jesus rise to the challenge of our cities? With evident love for the Lord and His Word, Jon Dennis skillfully helps us answer these questions with clear biblical exposition and straightforward applications, which spur on godly aspirations and zeal for the gospel. This book is well informed theologically and sociologically, yet practical and compelling. Wholeheartedly recommended."

Paul Harrison, Pastor, *Rue de Sèvres, Rue des Ternes*, Paris, France

"Jon Dennis has crafted a compelling vision for reaching and restoring our cities. He writes from Scripture, he writes from his heart, and he writes from his life. He and his family were already blessing our city day in and day out while so many of us were still just thinking about it. Read *Christ + City* and you will be inspired, equipped, and challenged to follow his lead."

Jon Ferguson, Founding Pastor, Chicago Network Leader, Community Christian Church; author, *The Big Idea, Exponential: How You and Your Friends Can Start a Missional Church Movement*, and *Discover Your Mission Now*

"Jon Dennis loves Chicago and the cities of the world—because such are what Christ loves. And in *Christ + City* he calls the church not to an Exodus but to a gospel-driven Eisodus back into the city. Pastor Dennis's years of experience since founding Holy Trinity Church and it's numerous congregations and ministries; his profound theological understanding of the church and its 'ultimate urban future'; and his knowledge of the modern city and the writings of the urban philosophers and theorists, have given us a book that is radically biblical and, therefore, prophetic and visionary. Between these covers lie nothing less than *the* essential strategy for world evangelization."

R. Kent Hughes, Senior Pastor Emeritus, College Church in Wheaton

"Jon has done a remarkable job of weaving the blessing and benefits of ministry in the city. He hits many of the difficulties head on with honesty and integrity. This is a great book for all Christians."

Wayne L. Gordon, founding pastor, Lawndale Community Church; President, Christian Community Development Association

CHRIST
+
CITY

CHRIST

+

CITY

Why the Greatest Need of the City
Is the Greatest News of All

JON M. DENNIS

∷ CROSSWAY®

WHEATON, ILLINOIS

Trade paperback ISBN: 978-1-4335-3687-8
PDF ISBN: 978-1-4335-3688-5
Mobipocket ISBN: 978-1-4335-3689-2
ePub ISBN: 978-1-4335-3690-8

Library of Congress Cataloging-in-Publication Data

Dennis, Jon M., 1966-
    Christ + city : why the greatest need of the city is the greatest news of all / Jon M. Dennis.
       p.   cm.
    Includes bibliographical references and index.
    ISBN 978-1-4335-3687-8
    1. City missions. 2. Cities and towns—Religious aspects—Christianity. I. Title. II. Title: Christ and city.
BV2653.D46   2013
266'.022—dc23   2012040405

Crossway is a publishing ministry of Good News Publishers.

VP		28	27	26	25	24	23	22	21	20	19	18
14	13	12	11	10	9	8	7	6	5	4	3	2

To Amy,
joyful companion
in the adventure with Christ

CONTENTS

INTRODUCTION

Awakening the Urban Generation

The greatest need of our day is for the gospel to enliven first our hearts, and then, our cities.

Which is to say that our most urgent calling is a gospel calling. It is *urban*—but it's not a call for new roads, better housing for the poor, bigger church buildings, or politicians with more integrity. It isn't a call for wiser city planning or even racial reconciliation. Our most urgent need today is for the gospel to awaken the urban generation.

My logic on this is straightforward:

1. Cities are filled with people whom God loves.
2. The gospel is the only message to save anyone anywhere.
3. Cities now represent more than half the world's population.
4. Cities are massively underrepresented by gospel-belief.

Don't get me wrong; I'm not saying we shouldn't send people with the gospel to all the ends of the earth. We should. If God is calling you to a faraway place, *go*. Unreached people everywhere need Christ.

I'm also not saying that rural people or suburbanites don't need Jesus. They do, as much as anyone.

And I'm certainly not saying that somehow, cities will save us. No: only Christ saves.

But I *am* saying that we have an unprecedented urban opportunity.

If the gospel penetrates our cities as never before, I believe we are *bound* to see racial reconciliation, greater compassion for the poor, and expanding church facilities (including house churches)—and, yes, even politicians with more integrity. I'm also convinced, perhaps counterintuitively, that as the gospel comes to cities in an unprecedented way, *the ends of the earth will hear the gospel more rapidly*. Why? Because when ethnic groups crowded into our cities are spiritually transformed, they'll make the effort to take this good news to the people groups nearest to them culturally, even though geographically distant.

AN URBAN MANIFESTO

This book is written to help intensify the picture of what it might look like for the gospel to penetrate our cities more deeply. I'm convinced that people want to know what it really means to follow Christ *anywhere*—including in the city. But beneath this lies their deeper desire, namely, to *glorify* Christ. Frequently in the rising rhetoric on urbanization, the city, rather than Christ, takes center stage. Our generation needs to grasp the importance of *Christ* for the city. Put differently: *Cities exist for Christ, not for us.*

The method of this book is to take a Scripture-spanning approach from Genesis to Revelation. Part 1 begins by looking forward to where we're going globally, and back to the first city. In part 2 we look at God's heart for the city and how a city is changed. Part 3 explores three key issues related to urban living, while part 4 points a way forward to keys for city change.

I'm not trying to address every single Scripture text on cities; generally, I'll take one passage at a time and examine it closely in context. And while this book isn't a "biblical theology of cities"—since the Bible isn't primarily about cities—I do want to provide a deeper understanding of the city biblically, theologically, and practically with Christ at the center.

In this book I'm really asking two questions:

1. *What would it look like to follow God more deeply and radically in the urban generation?*
2. *How should we think about cities in a God-centered, Christ-exalting way?*

I hope that this book, by God's grace, can be a kind of urban manifesto, a rallying cry for a new generation of global urban Christians who want to give themselves to a radical, gospel-centered, urban Christianity that spreads from city to city and to unreached regions beyond. My prayer is that gospel influence will grow in places like Paris, New York, Chicago, San Jose, Camden—and *your* city, regardless of its size. In this way we move nearer to Habakkuk's vision, revealed in a prophetic passage mingling judgment and salvation: "The earth will be filled with the knowledge of the glory of the LORD as the waters cover the sea" (Hab. 2:14).

As cities expand their power and sway, I want to see that very influence being leveraged for the gospel itself. In the subtitle for his book *Triumph of the City,* Harvard economist Edward L. Glaeser calls cities "our greatest invention," one that makes us "richer, smarter, greener, healthier and happier." I want to see this great invention stirring this generation to live for Christ.

At times in these pages you may think I'm writing rather optimistically. If so, it's because I believe God raised Jesus from the dead and is going to renew all things. You may also decide at times that I'm being pessimistic; this is because I take seriously human fallenness, what the biblical authors call sin. Both viewpoints come together, I'm convinced, in God's full perspective on humanity and, in particular here, on cities.

WHO SHOULD READ THIS BOOK?

This book is for anyone who wants to follow God more deeply and radically in this urban generation. It's written to show everyone—urbanite or non-urbanite, Christian or skeptic, single or married, city-lover or city-hater—a vision for growing spiritually at the flickering dawn of the urban age.

The main audience is the next generation of urban Christians. These are city-dwellers—and some not-yet city-dwellers—whom God is now calling to joyfully join a global-urban gospel movement. Some are young, eager, new Christians. Others are faithful pastors and leaders.

This audience includes those who are beginning to love the diversity, opportunities, architecture, culture, and food of the urban experience, even while perhaps hating other parts—the traffic, the busyness, the alienation. But more than anything else, they've fallen in love with the supremacy of Jesus Christ, the Lord and Savior of the city. Their growing vision is to spread his glory—to magnify the beauty and perfection of all his attributes—in cities small and great. They want to see his renewing love sweep with never-before-seen force across urban landscapes until these cities more fully reflect the kingdom of God. Their prayer is,

"Your kingdom come, your will be done on earth as it is in heaven"—or as it has recently been recast, "in my city as it is in heaven."

Recently I received an e-mail from one of these young Christians. He's a young married graphic designer here in Chicago, and for several months he had struggled with where God was calling him and his wife to live and work. He received a job offer from a reputable and prestigious employer in the suburbs. Then he wrote to say that "after a long two weeks of prayer and conversation with each other," he and his wife had decided to stay in Chicago. "The opportunity was pretty sweet," he acknowledged, "but we ultimately felt that it wasn't in line with our desire to be a part of a growing community in the city."

So I write for this couple—and for others in their generation who want to live in, raise children in, build houses in, and seek the welfare of the city. This includes my brothers and sisters who are part of God's remarkable movement called Holy Trinity Church, here in Chicago. It also includes the global leaders, brothers, and sisters in the widespread city-of-God and city-renewal initiative that the Spirit seems to be stirring up in cities around the world, particularly with influence from leaders such as Tim Keller. I've personally been encouraged by friends and leaders in New York, St. Louis, Philadelphia, Washington DC, Austin, L.A., San Francisco, Memphis, Paris, Dublin, Singapore, and Nairobi. This group—enlivened by the gospel—might well be called awakened urbanites.

The second audience, after awakened urbanites, is believers who, though they may be living in an area that far outstrips the size of ancient cities, do not consider themselves urban. They may find cities to be a drain and may be skeptical about any emphasis on cities, but they nevertheless care deeply about God's global mission. Perhaps they'll never want to live in the city; they may well identify with Emerson's observation, "I always seem to suffer from loss of faith on entering cities";[1] they might even echo Rousseau's conclusion that "cities are the abyss of the human species."[2] Yet for the sake of God's kingdom, they'll openly appreciate a manifesto on the city's role in God's purposes. And with a deep desire to follow God more fully and radically, they'll meditate on these biblical texts with me.

I want to help both of these audiences—awakened urbanite and self-perceived non-urbanite—to follow Christ and to center him in the city as we journey together to "the city . . . whose designer and builder is God" (Heb. 11:10).

This book's third audience may be quite difficult to reach but still worth targeting. They're people that Camus saw and felt in Paris decades ago when he wrote, "Ah, *mon ami*, do you know what the solitary creature is like as he wanders in big cities?"[3] Such wandering urbanites are still present, still restless, still feeling displaced at times. Like Camus, they draw energy from the city yet do not perceive God's overarching purpose for them in the urban environment. They're thoughtful, reflective post-Christians or non-Christians who have rejected the institutional church without having seriously or fully grasped the gospel. Still, they search for hope and purpose in this world.

If those words describe you, I salute your openness to wrestling with God's Word and hearing something about God's heart for cities and his heart for you.

A fourth and final audience includes people already committed to the urban future—those who *think* urban, who enjoy books like Ed Glaeser's *Triumph of the City*, Richard Florida's *The Rise of the Creative Class*, and Saskia Sassen's *The Global City*[4] but would like to dig more deeply into the biblical perspective. If you're in this category, but your vision for the urban future is lacking the hope of the resurrection, then may your commitment to the city be enriched by the biblical vision presented in this book—and may you perhaps be sobered as well, as you consider the city's realism and brutality with a new perspective.

God is taking his followers to a Final City. My hope is that a Christ-centered view of the city will give all of us "steel in our bones" for the journey ahead. May God allow us to share the vision of cities "filled with the knowledge of the glory of the LORD as the waters cover the sea" (Hab. 2:14).

Whatever your interests, wherever you live, I invite and challenge you to follow God deeply at the dawn of the urban age. May God awaken the urban generation!

PART 1

FOUNDATIONS OF CITY UNDERSTANDING

Our Direction

And I saw the holy city, new Jerusalem . . .

REVELATION 21:2

1

WHERE ARE WE GOING?

What is the city but the people?
WILLIAM SHAKESPEARE

They desire a better country, that is, a heavenly one.
Therefore God . . . has prepared for them a city.
HEBREWS 11:16

The urban generation has arrived. The city is not just here to stay—it's here to swell.

The experts agree: the human condition, which has become increasingly urban in recent decades, will only grow more so in decades to come, everywhere around the world.

Picture it: at some point in the past five years, a particular moment came when you and I and our fellow earth-inhabitants reached an epic milestone. In that instant—with the cry of a newborn child in Beijing, or when the feet of some migrant stepped over a boundary into Mumbai to start searching for a new home in the city—urban dwellers became a majority of the earth's population for the first time in this planet's long history.[1]

According to UN calculations and estimates, just forty years ago urbanites accounted for less than a third of the world's people. And in only forty more years they'll be over two-thirds—with the rate still rising.[2]

Where is our world going?

A GRIPPING QUESTION

A number of years ago, Rebekah was animated for months by that same question, scaled down personally: where am I going? And it eventually changed the trajectory of her life.

For her, the question was more specifically, "Is God calling me to the city? Is he asking my husband and me to move with our children to join in his urban movement?" The question wouldn't release its grip on them.

Rebekah had lived in cities before—New York and Chicago. Even her current location could have been called a city. But she wondered, "Why move to a much larger city *now*, leaving friends, when the kids had good schools ahead of them?" Sure, there was a romantic appeal of adventure about the idea. And yes, there were others joining a core group to plant a new church in a large city. But the question for Rebekah was more personal, more critical: "Is *God* doing something here? Is this *his* idea?" So Rebekah and her husband searched—praying, asking, probing: "God, is this you?"

One Sunday evening, hearing a message from the book of Jonah seemed to seal the deal, letting her know that *yes*, she *was* called to go. Turning away from that calling would be too costly. She and her husband were to give their lives as Christ-following adventurers, seeking the awakening of the urban generation.

It's a question worth asking for all of us. Where are we headed? And what, if anything, does the *city* have to do with it?

It's also a worthy question to ask about our culture, in an age that manifests an overarching sense of aimlessness. Many people sense a loss of direction and purpose. For all their hustle and busyness, they wonder, "Are we *really* going somewhere?" The question confronts them in their relationships and their careers, as well as in those moments when they look up and wonder about history itself. What exact destination is it all moving toward?

THE RISE OF URBAN INFLUENCE

On a practical level at least, it's hard to ignore the urban aspect of that future destination. For while urban areas keep claiming an increasingly greater percentage of the population, urban *influence* and *power* is expected to grow at an even faster rate. "The age of nations is over," announces international relations expert Parag Khanna; "the new urban age has begun." In an article in *Foreign Policy* magazine, Khanna writes this:

> The 21st century will be dominated not by America or China, Brazil or India, but by the city. In an age that appears increasingly unmanage-

able, cities rather than states are becoming the islands of governance on which the future world order will be built.[3]

Khanna (whose latest book is boldly titled *How to Run the World*) sees the urban scene as the arena where our planet's destiny is being decided:

> Cities . . . are the true daily test of whether we can build a better future or are heading toward a dystopian nightmare. . . .
>
> What happens in our cities, simply put, matters more than what happens anywhere else.[4]

PROGRESS OR DECLINE?

So where will our cities lead us? Some are pessimistic about our urban future; others hold an idealistic view.

Take urban theorist and author Mike Davis. In his recent book *Planet of Slums*, he notes that in much of the world the expansion rate of slums is far greater than the overall urban growth rate, leaving a less-than-pretty picture:

> Thus, the cities of the future, rather than being made out of glass and steel as envisioned by earlier generations of urbanists, are instead largely constructed out of crude brick, straw, recycled plastic, cement blocks, and scrap wood. Instead of cities of light soaring toward heaven, much of the twenty-first century urban world squats in squalor, surrounded by pollution, excrement, and decay.[5]

With the inhabitants of these places possessing little or no hope for productive, uplifting jobs as they struggle to survive, Davis sees these vast, polluted, crime-filled slums as seething volcanoes waiting to erupt in mob violence—"the distinctive battlespace of the twenty-first century."[6]

Others, however, prefer to see the vast swelling cities as not only our future's biggest reality but also our future's greatest hope.

To catch a high-spirited plug for city life, it's hard to beat Ed Glaeser's *The Triumph of the City: How Our Greatest Invention Makes Us Richer, Smarter, Greener, Healthier, and Happier*. In this upbeat and popular 2011 book, Glaeser—born and raised in Manhattan, and now an urban economist at Harvard—views cities past and present as being "engines of innovation" and "the places where their nation's genius is most fully expressed":

> The great prosperity of contemporary London and Bangalore and Tokyo comes from their ability to produce new thinking. Wandering these cities—whether down cobblestone sidewalks or grid-cutting cross streets, around roundabouts or under freeways—is to study nothing less than human progress.[7]

Glaeser acknowledges that such "urban splendor" coexists with "urban squalor":

> As many of us know from personal experience, sometimes city roads are paved to hell. The city may win, but too often its citizens seem to lose. . . . For every Fifth Avenue, there's a Mumbai slum; for every Sorbonne, there's a D.C. high school guarded by metal detectors.

But Glaeser also observes that "cities don't *make* people poor; they *attract* poor people. The flow of less advantaged people into cities from Rio to Rotterdam demonstrates urban strength, not weakness."

It's that urban strength, he says, that's bringing together all kinds of people into a heightened experience of productivity and prosperity: "Cities . . . are proximity, density, closeness. They enable us to work and play together, and their success depends on the demand for physical connection." Glaeser speaks of "the knowledge that is best produced by people in close proximity to other people," and observes how "cities speed innovation by connecting their smart inhabitants to each other" while also serving as "gateways between markets and cultures."

OUR TRUE DESTINATION

So, what are we to make of this urban trajectory?

Perhaps what's needed, first of all, is the profound and foundational understanding from God that *yes*, we are indeed going somewhere. That's what the Scriptures inform us. It's a destination that informs all UN projections as well as all personal life callings; it embraces the cry of the newborn urbanite and the journey of the migrant worker.

It's an *eschatological* reality, a final and ultimate destination, heavenly and everlasting—yet inescapably connected with everything in the here and now.

This linked reality was reflected in the classic ancient work *The City of God* by Augustine, where he so effectively contrasted the earthly and the heavenly, while also noting that both "are in this present world commingled, and as it were entangled together."[8]

To help us begin thinking about the intersection between Christ and city—particularly to reorient ourselves to see Christ positioned as central to the city and all things—there's one place that makes the most sense to begin: John's final vision of all things, a vision we see in the book of Revelation. As we meditate there on where we're going, perhaps we should orient ourselves *now* by where we are going *then*. As Thomas Merton writes in a twentieth-century introduction to *The City of God*,

> This eschatological view of history contemplates with joy the running out of the sands of time and looks forward with gladness to the Last Day that will make manifest the full glory of the "Whole Christ."[9]

A VISION FOR PEOPLE UNDER TRIAL

The book we know as Revelation was written to first-century Christians struggling under tremendous persecution. Their particular trials were inflicted most likely by Domitian, the Roman ruler who followed Nero. Nero's persecutions were notoriously vicious and capricious—the burning alive of followers of Christ, and crass sporting events in which Christians dressed in animal pelts had to face wild predators—but Domitian's torments were more systematic and widespread.

To these followers of Jesus near the end of the first century, John wrote his letter. The message is a transcendent vision of the risen and ruling Christ at the center of heaven, who will bring not only the judgment of Satan and the fall of "Babylon the Great" but also the arrival of an entirely new reality.

For modern readers, Revelation can feel a bit bizarre. It's a unique mix of apocalyptic-prophetic literature similar to portions of the biblical books of Daniel and Ezekiel, but it also takes the form of an epistle, a kind of personal letter. Penned by Jesus' beloved but exiled disciple

John from the island of Patmos, Revelation is intended to provide hope for the suffering church.

The lessons of Revelation on following God with faithfulness are just as relevant today as they were two thousand years ago. Our urban generation needs an enduring picture that transcends the here and now—that we might live faithfully within the here and now. Like ancient sailors who would often set their sights on a star to help guide their ship, John's vision of a new city in Revelation 21 tells us where all history is going.

TEMPORARY CITIES

From his island on Patmos, John writes,

> Then I saw a new heaven and a new earth, for the first heaven and the first earth had passed away, and the sea was no more. And I saw the holy city, new Jerusalem, coming down out of heaven from God. (Rev. 21:1–2)

One of the first things John's vision calls us to realize is that where we live *now*, compared to heaven, is a mere wisp.

A mistake we all make—no matter where we live—is to sacralize our homes. Removed as most of us are in this technological modern generation in the West from the severe suffering of the first century, we can become overly content with *this* world. Our "iEverythings" soften us. But John reminds us that all our devices and cities, all our rural farmlands, and all we treasure in them, will pass away. The vast cornfields of Iowa; the extensive vineyards along the California coast; Washington, DC's monuments and memorials—all will one day be no more. The lights on the Eiffel Tower in Paris will one day be permanently extinguished. My little neighborhood joint called Pizza Capri will be gone. No more. The urbanite's tiny backyard patch of grass, the suburbanite's large garden, and the farmer's acres of fields and pastures will all be swept away. John even says that the "sea"—a place that in Revelation symbolizes chaos and disorder and even rebellion—will be "no more."

Right at the beginning of our journey into understanding what it means to be awakened urbanites, finding our way to the permanent city—as we commit ourselves to follow God more radically—John reminds us: it will all be gone one day.

This means that no earthly city is final. Our cities are temporary. This is critical for awakened urbanites to grasp, because while it's right that we should work for our city's good (as we'll see), we're to hold on loosely, knowing that "the world is passing away" (1 John 2:17). God's Word reminds us that the kingdom of God—although *already*—is *not yet*. To use Augustine's language, we live now in the City of Man while seeking the City of God, knowing that only cataclysmic change will bring us home.

THE PERMANENT CITY

But comfortingly, all reality will be replaced with a new city.

John writes, "And I saw the holy city, new Jerusalem, coming down out of heaven from God" (Rev. 21:2). The description of the city is precise—it will be a *new* Jerusalem. John uses biblical imagery of Jerusalem, the famous city of David from the Old Testament, but calls it *new*.

Throughout the historical books, on into the Psalms, and then in the prophetic writings, the city of David symbolized the place of God's presence and favor. The psalmist calls Jerusalem, often referred to as Zion, the "joy of all the earth" (Ps. 48:2). It's the place David initially captured and where he then reigned for thirty-three years (2 Sam. 5:5). It's also the place where the Messiah, God's Son, is pictured as reigning over all people (Ps. 2:6; 9:11).

Destroyed by the Babylonians in the sixth century BC, and later rebuilt to a shadow of its previous glory by Nehemiah and others, the picture of Jerusalem in the prophets grows increasingly important and eternal—as well as urgent. In Isaiah we read of a trumpet blowing and of people once "lost in the land of Assyria" now returning to worship in Jerusalem (Isa. 27:13). We see Jerusalem portrayed as a place to dwell without weeping (30:19), and as an "immovable tent, whose stakes will never be plucked up" (33:20).

Isaiah envisions this beautiful new Jerusalem as awaking from a deep slumber:

> Awake, awake,
>   put on your strength, O Zion;

put on your beautiful garments,
     O Jerusalem, the holy city;
for there shall no more come into you
     the uncircumcised and the unclean.
Shake yourself from the dust and arise;
     be seated, O Jerusalem;
loose the bonds from your neck,
     O captive daughter of Zion. (Isa. 52:1–2)

Once awake, Jerusalem should burst with joy:

Break forth together into singing,
     you waste places of Jerusalem,
for the LORD has comforted his people;
     he has redeemed Jerusalem. (52:9)

Then this awakened and joyful city, freshly created along with a new heavens and earth, will become the place where God himself will rejoice:

For behold, I create new heavens
     and a new earth,
and the former things shall not be remembered
     or come into mind.
But be glad and rejoice forever
     in that which I create;
for behold, I create Jerusalem to be a joy,
     and her people to be a gladness.
I will rejoice in Jerusalem
     and be glad in my people;
no more shall be heard in it the sound of weeping
     and the cry of distress. (Isa. 65:17–19)

For a suffering and afflicted ancient Christian—as well as a technologically dazzled modern one—the new Jerusalem is to be a source of joy.

Drawing upon the rich biblical imagery of a new Jerusalem as the place of God's unfettered blessing and joy, John's vision in Revelation speaks of when comfort will come.

In a sense, this City of God follows the trajectory of the person of Jesus himself. Our Savior did not simply create a new humanity out of existing humanity. He was crucified, dead, and risen. His earthly body was transformed through a resurrection reality. And so, even as Christ has died, so the present heavens and earth will pass away, to be replaced by a new heaven and earth. It's as if the entire cosmos follows the Son of God through death and into resurrection. And when the new "resurrection" body of the heavens and the earth appears, a new city is born, cascading down out of heaven.

WHAT WE LONG FOR

Jean-Paul Sartre once expressed well the dilemma of conflicted modern man: "That God does not exist, I cannot deny; that my whole being cries out for God, I cannot forget." If we are honest, we do cry out for God. John's Apocalypse presents the arrival of this God we long for. God, who is undeniably *existent*, invites us to an intimacy that is unsurpassed. John sees "the holy city, new Jerusalem, coming down out of heaven from God"; then, with a carefully chosen image, he adds this description: "prepared as a bride adorned for her husband" (Rev. 21:2).

You see, throughout the Scriptures, God speaks of his relationship with his people as marital. Why? Because it's the deepest human intimacy possible.

John is again drawing on a rich Old Testament history when he speaks of the city as a bride. The prophets—in Ezekiel 16, for instance— often spoke of Jerusalem as a young girl, seen at a marriageable age as one whom God clothed and with whom he made a covenant. In the Old Testament imagery, however, God's bride turns away, commits adultery, and spurns her husband's love.

In Revelation, John describes the new city as one "prepared" as a bride adorned. He's speaking of wedding garments. He's describing the care in preparing for a wedding.

Think of the last wedding you attended. Hours were spent by bride and groom preparing. Invitations mailed. Tuxedos chosen. Hair arranged. All is made ready. Then that moment when the bride enters and the crowd rises to their feet. All eyes turn, led by the mother of the bride, to see the one who has adorned and prepared herself for this moment. She stands there in beauty.

Marriage means intimacy. John wants embattled Christians, those tempted to give up the fight, and distracted followers of Christ, to think of—even to long for—the moment when they'll rise to their feet—and meet God face to face.

For the urban generation to follow God more radically and deeply, the temporariness of this world and the blazing promise of what's ahead must be etched into our minds. The arrival of God's new city will bring about an indescribably rich intimacy between the Creator of all things and the people he has created and redeemed, an intimacy so profound that it will exceed the intimacy of even the purest and most powerful marriages on earth.

God promises that our eternal encounter with God will be like a wedding feast:

> Let us rejoice and exult
>   and give him the glory,
> for the marriage of the Lamb has come,
>   and his Bride has made herself ready;
> it was granted her to clothe herself
>   with fine linen, bright and pure"—
>
> for the fine linen is the righteous deeds of the saints.
>   And the angel said to me, "Write this: Blessed are those who are invited to *the marriage supper of the Lamb.*" (Rev. 19:7–9)

Heaven will be filled with rejoicing *in* God and exulting *of* God. God's people will glorify him, having been prepared for radical celebration and intimacy with him. *And you're invited!*

Augustine says it this way:

> Certainly that city shall have no greater joy than the celebration of the grace of Christ, who redeemed us by his blood. There shall be accomplished the words of the psalm, "Be still and know that I am God."[10]

WHERE GOD LIVES

But we haven't even touched on one of the most important truths for awakened urbanites to take away from John's vision: God *lives* in this city.

After the new city comes down from heaven, we read,

And I heard a loud voice from the throne saying, "Behold, the dwelling place of God is with man. He will dwell with them, and they will be his people, and God himself will be with them as their God." (Rev. 21:3)

This is what all the imagery of Jerusalem—throughout biblical history—has been telling us. The new Jerusalem, the final destination of God's people, will also be God's home. This is a stunning statement. Elsewhere the Bible says that even *to look on God* would cause us to die. When Moses asks to see God's glory, God tells him, "You cannot see my face, for man shall not see me and live" (Ex. 33:20). But for suffering disciples and awakened urbanites, our nearness to God will surpass even what was experienced in the beginning in the garden, when Adam and Eve "heard the sound of the LORD God walking in the garden in the cool of the day" (Gen. 3:8). Somehow, life in the new city will include not only feasting, rejoicing, and exulting, but also *dwelling with* the holy, almighty Creator.

Hear the proclamation again: "Behold, the dwelling place of God is with man." God will not be *above* man, not *against* us, not *over* us—but *with* us. It's too much to fathom.

No matter where you live—in the jungles of Sumatra, along the rocky shores of New England, or in view of the Golden Gate Bridge—no neighborhood can boast what the new Jerusalem can. Though God exists everywhere and fills all things, in the New Jerusalem *he will dwell with his people.* The journey of the awakened urbanite has its final destination with God.

TOTAL RENEWAL

This should be a comfort to us. Not only will God be present, but suffering—the suffering experienced by John's first readers and by everyone since—will be absent. The loud voice John hears announcing God's dwelling place with humanity also declares something else about him:

He will wipe away every tear from their eyes, and death shall be no more, neither shall there be mourning, nor crying, nor pain anymore, for the former things have passed away. (Rev. 21:4)

No matter what city or countryside you travel to—Kuala Lumpur or London, Cairo or Caracas, Toronto or Tokyo—there you'll find death and tears.

The recent book *Half the Sky,* coauthored by *New York Times* columnist Nicholas Kristof and his wife, Sheryl WuDunn, focuses on one particular horror in today's world involving both tears and death: the epidemic abuse of women. They tell of a young Cambodian girl who became a victim of sexual enslavement, modern-day sex trafficking.

> Srey Rath is a self-confident Cambodian teenager whose black hair tumbles over a round, light brown face. She is in a crowded street market, standing beside a pushcart and telling her story calmly, with detachment. The only hint of anxiety or trauma is the way she often pushes her hair from in front of her black eyes, perhaps a nervous tic. . . .
>
> Rath is short and small-boned, pretty, vibrant, and bubbly, a wisp of a girl whose negligible stature contrasts with an outsized and outgoing personality. . . . But Rath's attractiveness and winning personality are perilous bounties for a rural Cambodian girl. . . .
>
> When Rath was fifteen, her family ran out of money, so she decided to go work as a dishwasher in Thailand for two months to help pay the bills.[11]

As the girl's story unfolds, she is handed to a gangster known as "the boss," who takes her to Kuala Lumpur, Malaysia, where he runs a brothel. When she refuses to "work," he and others rape her, then tell her she must work to pay off the debt before she will be freed. While they punch her, she is told, "You have to serve the customers. If not, we will beat you to death. Do you want that?"

Eventually, Rath is forced to swallow a pill that the gangsters refer to as "the happy drug," which "made her head shake and induced lethargy, happiness, and compliance." Kept naked so she would not escape, Rath nevertheless eventually found a way to flee.

I share this story because, in the day of renewal, God will put an end to such abuse.

The awakened urbanite has a hope that is not merely personal, but social. Who could not long for such a day? Kristof and WuDunn write,

> The global statistics on the abuse of girls are numbing. It appears that more girls have been killed in the last fifty years, precisely because they were girls, than men were killed in all the battles of the twentieth century. More girls are killed in this routine "gendercide" in any one

decade than people were slaughtered in all the genocides of the twentieth century.[12]

Freedom from tragedies of this kind and of every kind is part of what the new city brings. It's a place entirely liberated from the horror of abuse and every other horror.

This is important to grasp. Neither our urban idealism nor any kind of cooperative human effort can ever produce this city.

One of the central promises of the gospel is that a day is coming when the piercing ache of death will be removed. Our hope for this is what allows Paul to say in triumph:

> Death is swallowed up in victory.
> O death, where is your victory?
> O death, where is your sting? (1 Cor. 15:54–55)

The arrival of the new city means a reversal. Pain, death, suffering, and abuse will all be removed, and *God will make all things right*. Mourning, crying, and pain—along with the squalor of slums with their pollution, excrement, and decay—will no longer exist, for the voice from the throne assures us, "the former things have passed away" (Rev. 21:4). It's not just the first heavens and the first earth that pass away—it's everything associated with them that is stained by death. The pain of a mother finding out her child has tumors will pass away. The sting of a disrespectful and domineering husband will be removed. The disappointment in not achieving a vocational dream will be reworked by God's grace. The pain of lovelessness or rejection. Of Alzheimer's, or jealousy, or hatred, or envy—these things will pass away.

Even more profound than the removal of everything negative is the fact that all these things will actually be *replaced*. John writes,

> And he who was seated on the throne said, "Behold, I am making all things new." (Rev. 21:5)

Not just *some* things new, but *all* things.

We sometimes joke that Chicago has two seasons, winter and construction. John is saying that in the new city, all things—every bridge, building, road—all is newly constructed and finished. *You* will be new. Your body will be new. Everyone around you will be new. *Nothing* will be outside the circle of "all things new."

No one will be in the new city unless that person is changed by the gospel and made new as well. Those who dwell in the new city always know that Christ on the cross has paid the penalty for their sin, and so they join in singing to him with all heaven's worshipers,

> Worthy are you . . .
> for you were slain, and by your blood you ransomed people for God
>   from every tribe and language and people and nation. (Rev. 5:9)

If you've been bought by the blood of Jesus, you're *in*—you're there in the new city, though you've been sexually immoral, or a murderer, or a liar, or a coward, or faithless, or an idolater. All those ransomed by the blood of Christ will be there.

As for the unrepentant others—their place, Jesus affirms, "is in the lake that burns with fire and sulfur, which is the second death" (Rev. 21:8). God's Word pictures two final destinations: one in keeping with Jesus' prolific teachings on hell, the other in his eternal presence. Those who reject Christ's teachings and his work for our salvation must fear hell's judgment.[13]

YOUR VISION

Let me close this chapter with a question: What dream, or vision, are *you* living? John has given us a powerful vision of the future, an urban vision of God. What's yours?

If we're honest, many North Americans are living only the American dream: grow up, make money, get married, raise children, buy a house, have a yard. It's a nice dream—but not God's dream. It can never be the ultimate destination for your life. In fact, the American dream—without the cleansing blood of Jesus—actually ends up in the lake of fire.

God has a different destiny for you. His vision for your life is that you join in the global urban movement of God toward the final city, the New Jerusalem. Where the current world is going globally, sociologically, and historically is matched by where the church is going eschatologically: toward a *city*.

Let the truth saturate your mind and heart: God is preparing a renewed city to replace all of existing reality. And if you are in Christ, your future is gloriously urban. The heavenly city is the final reality; "the island of governance on which the future world order will be built" is the city that comes down out of heaven.

So my invitation to you in this book is simple. *Join in where God is moving.* Whether your city is large or small, or even if God doesn't lead you to live in a city, you can still view cities as strategically and missiologically important, as people everywhere are drawn to them. Ray Bakke says it this way:

> The numbers are staggering—but so is the kaleidoscopic complexity of the cities. The city is like an escalator moving in the wrong direction— like a gigantic magnet, sucking people from jungles and from islands and from tribal groups.[14]

That is what's happening demographically.

So even if you don't live in the city, grasp the fact that cities have a massive strategic importance in the twenty-first century.

But again, more important than grasping this is your call to join God's urban movement personally and eschatologically—and, as necessary, *to repent.* Throw your idols and trophies before the One seated upon the throne, and turn to him. Grasp the destiny of what he's building—the new city—and put all your hopes there, and not in the American dream.

Take your part in the apocalyptic vision, as revealed to John and to us. A new reality, a new intimacy, a new dwelling place. *All things new.*

May this be the vision for your life and mine, and for all of Christ's church in every city throughout the world.

A CLOSING PRAYER

Father in heaven,

We would like to follow you more radically and deeply. We admit that often our view of the cities of the world with their glass and steel or their crude bricks and recycled plastic seem more real to us than the extravagant vision which is ahead. We repent of this. Help us to see the weary temporariness of this world; etch the blazing promise of what's ahead into our vision. Help us to see Christ at the center of the city to come.

Father, forgive us that often our dreams and our visions are for this world, not the next. We admit that we get consumed with and driven by our own dreams and visions—for our lives, our vocations, our careers, our marriages, our children. Thank you that one day you will wipe away every tear—all suffering. We look forward to that day. Thank you for showing us what John saw—the apocalyptic vision—and letting us know where you're taking us.

We pray that we would follow you with confidence and excitement, knowing these promises are true and safe and trustworthy—that they're as good as done, that even as Christ has risen from the dead, so one day a new city will appear.

We ask that you make clear your calling for us to be part of that great, global, urban future of your church.

In Christ's name we pray,

Amen.

2

AMBITION AND THE FIRST CITY

We live in the age of the city. The city is everything to us—
it consumes us, and for that reason we glorify it.

NIGERIAN SCHOLAR ONOOKOME OKOME

He has shown strength with his arm;
he has scattered the proud in the thoughts of their hearts.

MARY, MOTHER OF JESUS, IN LUKE 1:51

It would have been the tallest building in the Western hemisphere and one of the most distinctively elegant skyscrapers in the world. Rising above the confluence of the Chicago River and Lake Michigan, the Chicago Spire was to be a slender, spiraling, gracefully tapering shaft soaring skyward—all the while "redefining the form of the American skyscraper."[1] With its trimness and intricately achieved spiral (each floor was rotated slightly from the one beneath), many compared it to a gigantic upthrust drill bit boring a hole in the heavens. But no drill bit could ever boast of such beauty—the tower's perfect tapering would make it an aesthetic triumph.

The Chicago Spire was to reach up more than a third of a mile, 150 stories high. It would overshadow the Chicago skyline, ascending forty-eight stories higher than the Empire State Building in Manhattan, and in Chicago, forty stories higher than the Sears Tower (now the Willis Tower), fifty higher than the John Hancock Center, and fifty-four higher than the Trump Tower. Entirely residential, it would contain almost 1,200 dwellings. At the top, a two-story, 10,000-square-foot penthouse would be the world's loftiest home.

This was an international project, designed by Spanish architectural superstar Santiago Calatrava and pushed toward actualization by Irish developer Garrett Kelleher. But it would also be distinctively Chicagoan, an icon of what the city is all about: bold aspiration and confidence, magnificent muscle and might, and clean, daring artistry.

When the planned project was announced, it quickly won support from the city government and enthusiasm from ordinary Chicagoans. Construction began in the summer of 2007 on the massive underground supporting structure for the spire. Then suddenly, worldwide economic turmoil the following year put the brakes on the project. New York, Dubai, Nanjing, Jakarta, and cities across the world at the time put their building plans on hold.[2]

The initial construction schedule called for completion in 2012. But drive by the site now, and instead of staring up at a soaring, shimmering tower parting the clouds, you look down into a 76-foot hole in the ground.

WHY ARE WE HERE?

Chicago, home of the world's first skyscraper, has always been a city reaching up, making a name for itself, a city that builds and rebuilds and invents and reinvents. That's been true of cities throughout history. People come to be part of that dynamic as they seek to make their mark. The general idea is that together, in this energetic and creative and resourceful environment, we can accomplish more—for ourselves individually, but also together.

Urban studies theorist Richard Florida, author of *The Rise of the Creative Class* and *Cities and the Creative Class*, has specialized in tracing the connection between human creativity and urban existence. Florida proposes that the most successful cities long-term are those able to attract talent by creating contexts that support imaginative and innovative urbanites—artists, "bohemians," and others.[3] He states, "Creativity has come to be the most highly prized commodity in our economy—and yet it is not a 'commodity.'"[4]

Of course, a great deal gets accomplished through the inspiration and vigor that drives today's cities. Every city has its monuments to human strength and ingenuity. But there are also plenty of endeavors large and small that end in frustration, like the Chicago Spire. What is rarely examined is what lies *beneath* our creativity, ingenuity, and ambition. As we think about the city, eventually we have to ask, "Why are we here? When we come to the city . . . *why* do we come?"

A provocative answer is suggested by Boris Johnson, the mayor of London. In an interview with *New York* magazine, he acknowledged how people come to the city for such things as opportunities, relationships, and wealth. "But above all," he noted, "talented people seek cities for fame. They can't get famous in the . . . village." He admitted, "That's what's driving me. That's the awful fact."

Johnson continued,

> A city, by the sheer concentration of people, provides the most amazing opportunity to get that affirmation—which is what it's about. The reason that so many ideas are produced in cities is not just that people are cross-fertilizing; it's because they want to beat each other. They want to become more famous than the other person.[5]

How far off the mark is the mayor's explanation? Would it actually be true for a significant number of urbanites today?

And how might God view humanity's pursuit of urban fame?

THE FIRST URBAN STORY

We saw in the previous chapter how the book of Revelation brings an urban climax to the story of mankind that had started so long ago in a garden. We saw that all of humanity is going either to the new city coming down out of heaven from God, or to a lake that burns with fire and sulfur. This urban ending for God's ransomed people can seem surprising to us, but the *city* theme actually arises early in the Bible's pages.

Genesis opens with God mightily speaking all things into being: "Let there be light!"—and so it is! He creates mankind and places them in that garden. Continuing to read, we quickly encounter the fall of mankind, followed by Cain's killing of his brother Abel, and then the explosive spread of mankind's corruption. Then comes the destruction of humanity through a catastrophic flood, through which only Noah and his family are saved—and there's a new beginning.

We come then, in chapters 10 and 11, to a listing of the tribes and nations descended from Noah and his sons, and an account of how they spread far and wide.

Dropped into the middle of this "table of nations," nestled in the opening verses of Genesis 11, is the remarkable story of the Tower of Babel. It's a story of human creativity in the first "global city," and of God's ability to reveal the misdirected ambition beneath that creativity.

The story also marks a turning point in Scripture. Immediately after these events at Babel, God sets in motion his plan to bless "all the families of the earth" through Abram (later called Abraham), a man from whom Jesus Christ would eventually descend and bring this promise to fulfillment (Gen. 12:3; Matt. 1:2–16; Gal. 3:16).

Occupying such a strategic placement, the extraordinary account of Babel sounds forth its momentous message—one that we can't afford to miss as we seek God's view of the city.

The story begins:

> Now the whole earth had one language and the same words. And as people migrated from the east, they found a plain in the land of Shinar and settled there. (Gen. 11:1–2)

Intrigue builds already. *Shinar* is a name destined to become linked in Scripture with Babylon, the archetypal anti-God city (see Daniel 1:2).

Meanwhile, in the minds and hearts of these pioneers on the plains of Shinar, a plan takes shape:

> And they said to one another, "Come, let us make bricks, and burn them thoroughly." And they had brick for stone, and bitumen for mortar. Then they said, "Come, let us build ourselves a city and a tower . . ." (Gen. 11:3–4)

Archaeology reveals to us the ancient Near Eastern structures known as ziggurats—multistory towers of tiered squares constructed of sun-dried or fire-burned bricks made from straw and mud and sealed with bitumen (think of tar or asphalt). A temple or shrine crowned the highest square, with long-ramped stairways leading up to it. It was intended to penetrate the heavens with its grandeur and prominence, thereby connecting earth to heaven.[6] It made the statement, "We do commerce with the gods!" This is almost certainly the design being pursued here by Shinar's architects and structural engineers.

This building project they conspire to complete is huge, encompassing not only "a tower" but also "a city." And their collective motive, we quickly discover, is even larger, something vast and deep:

> Come, let us build ourselves a city and a tower with its top in the heavens, and let us make a name for ourselves, lest we be dispersed over the face of the whole earth. (11:4)

Prideful ambition is driving this thing. We might call it the Human Achievement Project, and it's being pursued in separation from God and his will in at least two ways.

First, these people want somehow to avoid being dispersed throughout the world, very likely in opposition to God's prior command for humanity to "fill the earth" (Gen. 1:28; 9:1).[7] Rather than dispersing, they wanted to be together in one place. God intended this planet to be widely inhabited, but they weren't so sure they wanted to be a part of that.

Second, and more basic, the builders want to make a name for *themselves* rather than exalt God's name, the One who created heaven and earth. Their construction project is not primarily about harnessing technology to better serve mankind and meet its needs for shelter and community. It's about making a *name*, not making a building; it's all about *fame*. Calvin puts it starkly:

> Here we see their motive in this undertaking. Whatever else might happen, they wanted their names to be immortalized on earth. So they built as if they were opposing God's will. Ambition not only harms men but stands in proud opposition to God. To erect a citadel was not in itself so great a crime. But to raise an eternal monument to themselves that might endure throughout all ages showed headstrong pride as well as contempt for God.[8]

What they hope to build is something lofty enough and impressive enough that it can't escape lasting attention. It would seem like a miracle—with themselves esteemed as the miracle workers. "This," writes Calvin, "is the perpetual infatuation of the world. . . . [to] neglect heaven, and seek immortality on earth, where everything is fading and transient."[9]

From a modern perspective, there's something a bit humorous about these people in Shinar wanting to touch the heavens with a tower built from mud-bricks and tar. Our technology today is immeasurably advanced, our resources vastly multiplied, and the size and scope of our projects enormously expanded. What *hasn't* changed is the human heart and our natural tendency toward self-exaltation, to use everything around us as a kind of lever to lift up who we are.

As a small example, think of a phrase at a dinner party that subtly lets everyone know what you've accomplished or what you're like. Researchers at Harvard University recently reported that "talking about ourselves . . . triggers the same sensation of pleasure in the brain as food or money."[10] By nature we draw attention to ourselves; we're glory-hounds. Self-infatuation and the desire for greatness are alive and well, as epidemic as ever. By our attitudes and words and actions, we ourselves make the same declaration that resounded in Shinar: "Let us make a name for ourselves."

The concept of *name* in the Scriptures has to do with reputation, character, honor, recognition, distinction. Interestingly, just a few verses later, God gives Abram his promise to "make your name great," just as he later does with David (Gen. 12:2; 2 Sam. 7:9)—but this is on God's own terms, and in a way that brings him glory. God often in Scripture makes it clear that he alone will receive glory, that he is making a name for himself—"an *everlasting* name" (Isa. 63:12; see Ex. 14:17–18; Neh. 9:10; Dan. 9:15).

Throughout Scripture, the Lord's name is interchangeable with his repute, his glory. So the builders in Shinar are essentially saying, "Let's build *who we are* for all the world to see. Let's make ourselves renowned and celebrated. We have no need for God." This is why these aspiring urbanites have come to Babel.

Upon reflection, we might wonder, *So what's really wrong with that?* Why not let these tower builders have their fame? After all, didn't this project arise out of their own inventiveness and resourcefulness? And wouldn't it be their own sweat and muscles that would bring this thing into existence? Why not give them due credit for it?

But let's hear now from God in this story.

WHAT GOD SEES

It's clear to us what these people are doing, and why. Now the narrative brings God on the scene.

> And the LORD came down to see the city and the tower, which the children of man had built. (Gen. 11:5)

There is intended irony here. What seemed so immense in the people's imagination is actually so miniscule to the mind of God who reigns over all things that he must descend![11] Isaiah reminds us that God "sits above the circle of the earth, and its inhabitants are like grasshoppers" (Isa. 40:22). To God, the workers at Shinar—like our skyscraping cranes today—look smaller than insects.

The Lord's "coming down" to Babel is anthropomorphic language, helping us understand God's response by using the terminology of human actions and characteristics. This figure of speech depicts him in his heavenly vantage point stooping or crouching down to examine the scene at Shinar. It's almost as if what they're building there is so small, God has to hunker down on hands and knees to inspect it closer.

God's cosmic vision is something we often see in Scripture, as in these Psalms:

> . . . he looked down from his holy height;
> from heaven the LORD looked at the earth. (Ps. 102:19)
> The LORD looks down from heaven;
> he sees all the children of man. (Ps. 33:13)
> The LORD looks down from heaven on the children of man,
> to see if there are any who understand, who seek after God. (Ps. 14:2)

In the Babel story, the particular language "the LORD came down" speaks also of a contrast in direction—the people aspire upward, build upward, reach upward, but God is coming *down*. The people are craving to ascend; but God *descends*, in his attention and concern.

And what does he look down and see?

Again notice that both city *and* tower are mentioned. It's not just the "Shinar Spire" that's getting a divine examination here, but the urban center around it as well. Both city and tower had already taken shape enough to be recognizable for what they were designed to be. Before intervening, God seems to have waited until the work was quite advanced—perhaps for the reason, as Calvin observes, that "he might give the more decisive evidence of his judgment."[12]

And now the Lord speaks:

> And the LORD said, "Behold, they are one people, and they have all one language, and this is only the beginning of what they will do. And nothing that they propose to do will now be impossible for them." (Gen. 11:6)

There's a tone of humor in his voice. God isn't worried. As Calvin surmises, "There seems to me to be . . . a suppressed irony" in these words, as if it might take some trouble on God's part to deal with this situation.[13] "This is only the beginning," God says—of their arrogance and ambition, their basic human assumption that they're so full of brains and ability, there's no such thing as impossibilities. Into their own minds and their children's minds they will drill the maxim: *you can do it!*—always with a view toward making an ever-greater name for themselves. This prideful ambition is addicting and endless; there never comes a point where they finally say, "We're famous enough now; we can relax."

God decides to give the builders a reminder of who's really in charge—which is the real issue here. God, all-powerful, is in control of all things.

The divine speech continues:

> Come, let us go down and there confuse their language, so that they may not understand one another's speech." (11:7)

The plural way that this is expressed echoes the words of Genesis 1:26: "*Let us* make man in our image, after our likeness." We're hearing from the three Persons of the Trinity, and this connection to God's earlier statement reminds us of a basic truth: What fame could be greater, what identity could be more meaningful, than the simple glorious fact of being *created in the image of God*?

Here again the theme of God's downward movement recurs, emphasizing all the more his gracious condescension to humanity. And in so descending, what God chooses to *do* here is to diversify the people's tongues. At one time all human beings everywhere "had one language and the same words" (Gen. 11:1), but that reality was now forever defunct, splintered in a single moment.

The resulting confusion among the people leads to their scattering, and the narrative stresses God's responsibility for this:

> So the LORD dispersed them from there over the face of all the earth. (11:8)

The break-up that these people feared and tried to prevent (11:4) happens anyway, reminding us that "no wisdom, no understanding, no counsel can avail against the LORD" (Prov. 21:30). Yes, God is in control. His demonstration of that fact is doubly emphasized in the story's conclusion:

> . . . and they left off building the city. Therefore its name was called Babel, because there *the LORD* confused the language of all the earth. And from there *the LORD* dispersed them over the face of all the earth. (Gen. 11:8–9)

With fitting irony, the narrative details the lasting name for this place: *Babel,* meaning "confusion"—not at all the illustrious "name" which the builders had wanted to be remembered and celebrated forever. Yes, they got their name. Notice that it's the *city,* rather than the tower alone, that bears this name. In the Old Testament, Babel will come to equal Babylon, the one city in Scripture that most symbolizes the world's arrogant and wicked opposition to God.

Babel is the solitary name to endure from this episode, the only name known of all these people who so boldly asserted, "Come . . . let us make a name for ourselves" (Gen. 11:4).

WHY DO WE COME?

This story raises a question and a warning for the urban generation. *Why do we come to our cities? What are we working to achieve?* Some come to cities to study, whether it's finance or film or culinary arts school. Others come for relationship.

Babel tells us that God cares *why* we come. God cares deeply about the aspirations of the human heart. Babel reminds us that the most important project of all is not the sum total of our human building or straining, but our humility and dependence.

It would be easy to assume from Genesis 11 that God is against the city. But God is not anti-urban. God is anti-*pride*. One Bible scholar puts it this way:

> In and of itself, the construction of cities does not cause the Lord's displeasure; for example, Israel celebrates holy Jerusalem. Rather, God censures the human pride and security that people attach to cities (Gen. 4:12–14, 17).[14]

The confusion at Babel is more than the confusion of languages; it is the confusion of aims of life, confusion of how we please God.

> The Babelites, in their longing for a humanly constructed, human-glorifying city, earn for themselves the ignominious name "Confusion."[15]

This story presents a truth that we easily forget: All cities exist for God—his name, his purposes, his glory.

A CONTEXT OF CONTRAST

As we've mentioned, Babel's ambition in Genesis 11 is followed by the adventure and faith of Abram in Genesis 12—and the contrast between the two is interesting and intense.

While chapter 11 shows basic human pride driving mankind away from God in a project that ends in failure, chapter 12 introduces the Divine Achievement Project—initiated by God, and incapable of being overturned. God calls Abram to follow, and he does.

In Genesis 11 we observe the cursing and scattering of the ambitious many; in Genesis 12, from among all the people listed, we find the choosing of just one man for God's purposes—Abraham.

Forgetting God, the people in chapter 11 declare, "Let us *make a name* for ourselves." In chapter 12, God himself promises Abraham, "I will bless you and *make your name great*" (Gen. 12:2).

While ignoring God, the people in Genesis 11 labor to erect a city and tower as monuments to themselves. In Genesis 12, Abraham builds as well; we read twice that this consummate man of faith "built an altar to the LORD," and in worship he "called upon the name of the LORD" (Gen. 12:7–8). God's name is at the center of Abraham's life; Babel is at the center of the lives of the people of Shinar.

So at the collapse of the first urban generation, as God sends Abraham on his mission with the word "Go," this man shines with the one quality that pleases God: faith. In the New Testament, we learn more about both the man and the mission. We observe Abraham's trust:

> By faith Abraham obeyed when he was called to go out to a place that he was to receive as an inheritance. And he went out, not knowing where he was going. By faith he went to live in the land of promise, as in a foreign land, living in tents . . . (Heb. 11:8–9)

Abraham is the model for following God, no matter what generation we're in. He looks forward, and Hebrews tells us of the hoped-for destination that motivated him: "For he was looking forward to *the city that has foundations*, whose designer and builder is God" (11:10). God sent Abraham on a journey whose ultimate destination was the eternal city, the new city coming down out of heaven from God.

CITY OF MAN AND CITY OF GOD

Augustine began writing his monumental book *The City of God* precisely sixteen centuries ago. A short while earlier, in AD 410, the unthinkable had happened: Rome, the Eternal City, capital of an enduring empire, had been sacked by barbarians. The Roman empire, for centuries the greatest power on earth, was now collapsing all around. How could Rome, the glory of civilization, come to this? Many Romans blamed the decline on the weakness engendered by the rising influence of Christians and the neglect of Rome's ancient pagan gods.

Augustine set out to philosophically refute that notion. In his book, he wrote of two cities in conflict—the impermanent City of Man, confined to the cares and pleasures of earthly life, and the City of God, dedicated to eternal realities. Their lasting conflict, Augustine writes, was born out of opposite loves:

... two cities have been formed by two loves: the earthly by the love of self, even to the contempt of God; the heavenly by the love of God, even to the contempt of self. The former, in a word, glories in itself, the latter in the Lord. For the one seeks glory from men; but the greatest glory of the other is God, the witness of conscience. The one lifts up its head in its own glory; the other says to its God, "Thou art my glory, and the lifter up of mine head" [Ps. 3:3].[16]

Babel and Abraham show us these two loves. Abraham's life is one of following God, wherever he leads, to the Eternal City. Babel shows the folly of seeking only the earthly city, in contempt of God. As we meditate on following God in the urban generation, it's critical that we grasp the existence of both planes, these two contradictory directions, these two passionate pursuits opposed to each other. It's impossible to follow both at once, or to lift up both together. Love of ourselves and love of our name will always clash with the love of God and of his purposes.

Babel shows us well the model of self-love, self-glory, and contempt of God. It also clearly demonstrates that every ambition without humility, all self-centeredness without grace, and every Human Achievement Project separated from God's glory always ends in failure. We may view our pursuits—whether parenting or film-writing, fashion or plumbing—as majestic and grand and powerful in their scope and perception, but to God they're timid and tepid—and ultimately inconsequential, if opposed to him. All our human ambitions ultimately can be overruled by the God who sees our hearts. It's his actions that are final and definitive. In the end, only his purposes endure.

The City of Man is fragile and ultimately failing; it is shaken, scattered, overthrown. But there's another city, established by God for those who trust him, which is far more powerful and truly enduring.

This book of Augustine's "is global and all-encompassing," and in its day represented "nothing less than the beginnings of a new philosophy of history"; its point is clear: everything "is relentlessly moving toward the grand climax when God will judge the world and establish a new order."[17] That grand climax, that ultimate new order, is the City of God that Augustine wrote about, the descending heavenly city that John's eyes saw in Revelation, and the permanent city that an awakened Abraham trusted God for, even as he lived in tents.

GOD CAME DOWN

As we seek to follow God during the rise of the urban generation, we, like Abraham, need God to come down. No matter what empire we build, what careers we embark on, what seas we sail, what people we love, *nothing* will raise us into the heavens and out of this world. Only the gospel, meeting the city's greatest need, does that. The Son of God left the eternal city to call us, just as God called Abraham. To the urban generation Jesus says, "Follow!"

Since the time of Babel, countless more proud monuments to human ambition have been raised—not just edifices and municipalities, but also organizations and systems and social networks and scientific inventions and works of art, and much more. A great many of these have already disintegrated into dust and disarray, long ago forgotten; the rest will ultimately follow.

Whether we're building ourselves, our portfolios, our careers, or our relationships, the story of Babel points a finger to our heart and ambition and says, *Why?* Where is our real sense of security and safety, our meaning and fulfillment? What is our protection? Where is our power and confidence and strength? Only in *ourselves?*

In his great and majestic hymn "A Mighty Fortress Is Our God," Martin Luther says,

> Did we in our own strength confide,
>   our striving would be losing,
> were not the right man on our side,
>   the Man of God's own choosing.

The Man of God's own choosing, according to Luther and God's Word, is not Abraham, but Christ. To strive while trusting in our own strength ultimately brings only failure, never success.

The Babel story confirms for us that God is not disengaged from the work of this world or from our cities or from human ambition. While we attempt to reach up, he comes down. He sees all and controls all, and he intervenes whenever and wherever and however he chooses. He "came down" decisively in the permanent, everlasting person of Jesus. He still comes down with unlimited ability to disperse and scatter whatever we try to construct apart from him. Yet he also remains *above*—seated in the heavens, all-powerful and all-knowing—and with steadfast love that endures forever.

No spire, no city is ultimately safe, but "the name of the LORD is a strong tower; the righteous man runs into it and is safe" (Prov. 18:10). The tower we long for, that structure which can reach the heavens, is already built.

Man reaches up, in vain; but *God, in his grace, reaches down.* The Bible teaches that heaven has come down to us most wonderfully and assuredly in the person of Jesus Christ, to bring us back up to heaven. That is what the gospel tells us. And that, in fact, is what Revelation 21 is all about, as we glimpsed in the last chapter. Because of what Christ has done on the cross—paying the penalty for our sin, for our prideful ambition and our willful ignoring of God—we have open access to the very throne of God in the heavens. Because the human city reaching up will always fail, therefore in Christ the new city comes down.

And so we discover a truly worthy name to lift up, for "God has highly exalted him and bestowed on him the name that is above every name" (Phil. 2:9). The name of Jesus Christ is worthy of all glory, since "there is salvation in no one else, for there is no other name under heaven given among men by which we must be saved" (Acts 4:12).

The cross of Christ towers infinitely higher than Babel ever could.

As we learn to follow God in this urban generation, *his* is the name we lift up and exalt, not that of Nimrod or Abraham, or our own name, but only the eternal and matchless name of our Lord Jesus Christ. And as he walks with us in these very streets, through the presence of his Spirit . . . our cities, which exist for him, become a lever to lift up his name.

A CLOSING PRAYER

Our Father in heaven,

Your steadfast love, O Lord, extends to the heavens, your faithfulness to the clouds; your name is a mighty tower, a refuge for your people. You alone are our rock and salvation. We lift our hands up to you in praise. Who is like you, O Lord?

We thank you that, even as you dispersed the first urbanites in judg-

ment, by your Spirit, through the cross of Christ, you are calling people back to yourself.

Jesus Christ, we praise you for coming down and walking among us; dying that we might be raised again with you.

Spirit, we praise you for opening our eyes to the truth.

Cleanse us from our selfish ambitions; forgive us for when we want to make a name for ourselves; your name, O Lord, is a name to be revered, worshiped, and honored above every name. We praise you, in Christ's name,

Amen.

PART 2

GOD'S HEART FOR THE CITY

How Cities Change

Should I not pity Nineveh, that great city?

JONAH 4:11

3

PRAYER AND THE CITY

"I am afraid . . . I dare not look," whispered Alyosha.
"Do not fear Him. He is terrible in His greatness,
awful in His sublimity, but infinitely merciful."

FROM FYODOR DOSTOEVSKY'S *THE BROTHERS KARAMAZOV*

One of his disciples said to him,
"Lord, teach us to pray."

LUKE 11:1

Urban spirituality, some would say, is an oxymoron. They may have a point.

As we saw in the last chapter, the founding of the first city ended with God's powerful dispersal of its citizens. God, it might seem at first glance, must have something against cities.

In contrast, God seems to exalt nature; Scripture lifts it up as a means to summon our worship of him. "Let the field exult," the psalmist declares, "and everything in it! Then shall all the trees of the forest sing for joy before the LORD" (Ps. 96:11–12). The same track is followed in Isaiah: "Break forth into singing, O mountains, O forest, and every tree in it!" (Isa. 44:23). And when David sings about the blessedness God bestows, his lyrics often linger in a pastoral setting, as here:

The pastures of the wilderness overflow,
    the hills gird themselves with joy,
the meadows clothe themselves with flocks,
    the valleys deck themselves with grain,
        they shout and sing together for joy. (Ps. 65:12–13)

Such imagery is common in the Bible's pages. It's true that the city of Jerusalem, with its celebrated name *Zion*, is also frequently exalted in Scripture; such lofty recognition, however, is not for being urban, but simply because of God's presence as represented in the temple there (see Ps. 50:2; 132:13; 1 Kings 11:36).

What we *don't* see featured in Scripture is the urban landscape as a particular source of praise for God, or in the act of praising him. Rivers and forests are told to "clap their hands" (as in Ps. 98:8 or Isa. 55:12)—but such attribution is never given to crowded dwellings and market-places, or for skyscrapers and commuter-clogged freeways.

In *cities*—places where field and forest, meadow and mountain seem a world away—is it even possible to be deeply spiritual? In the human crush of the urban scene, can we actually pray and praise in the fullest intimacy with God that humanity can experience? *Can* we follow God, deeply and radically, in the urban environment?

Or does the very *humanness* of the city stifle our awe of God and even our sense of needing him at all? If the natural world that God created prompts praise for the Creator, does the human-designed and human-engineered architecture of the city draw attention only to humanity, while luring the soul's gaze away from God? Writing about New York City, author Eric Metaxas (himself a New Yorker) describes as "extraordinarily rare" any person who can "live, indeed thrive, amidst the inescapable din and the infinite enticements of this great city" and yet still "be a self-examined soul."[1]

Yet this is our task: to love and follow God with all our heart and soul and mind and strength, *in the city*, in this urban age. It calls for an intensity of prayer that transcends and overcomes the urban bustle and blast; it calls for prayer that cries out *in* the city, and *for* the city.

CITIES EXIST FOR GOD

One of the earliest points in the Bible where we witness prayer for a city comes in the story of Abraham, someone who knew God well. As we saw in the last chapter, God had selected him, out of all the vast realms of ancient people, to bring his blessings to "all the families of the earth" (Gen. 12:3)—a promise eventually fulfilled to the uttermost through Abraham's descendant Jesus (Gal. 3:16).

In Genesis 18, we see Abraham's heart moved with compassion for the notoriously wicked city of Sodom, a city destined for divine destruction. The Lord had confirmed that "the outcry against Sodom and Gomorrah is great and their sin is very grave" (Gen. 18:20). But Abraham pleads with God for the city, humbly and boldly.

"Will you indeed sweep away the righteous with the wicked?" he asks God. "Suppose there are fifty righteous within the city. Will you then sweep away the place and not spare it for the fifty righteous who are in it?" (18:23–24).

God answers that if he finds fifty righteous people there, he will indeed refrain from destroying the city.

Unsure of Sodom's uprightness, Abraham continues to press God, still with utmost humility. "Behold, I have undertaken to speak to the Lord," Abraham acknowledges, "I who am but dust and ashes" (18:27). But what if only forty-five righteous persons were found there—what then?

God responds, "I will not destroy it if I find forty-five there" (18:28).

Abraham continues his intercession, dropping the numbers of the righteous down to forty, then thirty, then twenty, then ten, always with the same assuring response from God.

You know what happens next. God destroys the entire city of Sodom, sparing only Abraham's nephew Lot and his family, though Lot's wife is turned to salt.

What are we to make of this terrifying picture of judgment, and of this preceding behavior from Abraham?

It's a reminder that we often invert the biblical perspective. In the modern mind, cities exist for *people*. Us. We build them, we run them. We do as we like in them. But as we were reminded in the last chapter, Scripture points out that *nothing*—cities included—exists primarily for us. Cities exist for God. For his glory. As all things do.

This passage makes no sense to us—and won't make sense to many modern people who can't bear to think of God as righteous—unless we see God as holy. Can God *love* the city if he *judges* the city? The answer is yes. But in a startling truth, God loves his glory more. As Abraham puts it, "Shall not the Judge of all the earth do what is just?" (Gen. 18:25). The implicit answer is yes. God as Judge *will* do what is just—for all our cities, not just Sodom.

TALKING, LAUGHING, ASKING QUESTIONS

Abraham in this episode gives us a model for praying—with a twist. His prayers are bold yet humble. He doesn't hesitate to ask for the city's salvation, but at the same time he surrenders to God: "I who am but dust and ashes" (18:27).

Besides being bold and humble, Abraham's prayers are intimate, interactive, and persistent. He talks with God as a man talks with another man, and God responds accordingly. I'm not saying we should expect to always hear God's verbal answers when we pray; I'm suggesting that prayer is *talking*.

Listening to Abraham's spoken words, we have the sense he *knows* God as a child knows a parent. In Leif Enger's award-winning novel *Peace Like a River*, there's a great moment when the eleven-year-old narrator, Reuben, recalls slipping by his father's door at night and overhearing him pray aloud—"talking, laughing, asking questions of the Lord as though it had been you or me . . . in there."[2] That's a view of prayer that I find comforting. In his book *A Praying Life*, Paul E. Miller demystifies prayer by pointing out that just saying "Father!" is a simple enough prayer.[3]

When Jesus teaches us to begin our prayer with "Our Father in heaven" (Matt. 6:9), he gives us a sense both of relational intimacy (*our Father*) as well as holiness (our Father *in heaven*).

Praying like children to their Father means telling God whatever is on our minds. Sometimes, as in Abraham's case, that will be the salvation of a city. At other times it will be smaller and simpler things.

Miller suggests that as we grow older, our childlike faith often "dies a thousand little deaths."[4] So he encourages, "Don't be embarrassed by how needy your heart is and how much it needs to cry out for grace. Just start praying."[5] He goes on, "Become like a child—ask, believe, and, yes, even play. When you stop trying to be an adult and get it right, prayer will just flow because God has done something remarkable. He's given you a new voice"[6]—that new voice being the Holy Spirit within.

For the awakened urbanite, prayer isn't a luxury; it's a lifeline. The pace and violence of the city is too intense, the temptations too powerful, the gritty disappointments too strong without a life of prayer.

There's no need for the spectacular—praying while bumping along on the bus can do, or while sitting in a coffee shop with scribbled journal in hand. Even then, what's really happening truly *is* spectacular: prayer ties us to *God*, looping a rope of communion to the foot of the throne.

NOT WEARY IN WELL DOING

Sometimes we find encouragement in our ordinary prayers by looking back on great movements of God.

Turn the clock back to 1857, to an old church on Fulton Street in New York City. A man is there, alone, praying on his knees. His name is Jeremiah Lanphier, and he's just a businessman. "Just" is no slight; it's to say that an extraordinary move of God in 1857 came about not through some urban pope carried on a silk-covered sedan chair upheld by footmen, or by some monk dressed in burlap, or by some pinch-collared cleric, but through a man accustomed to the hurly-burly of the business world.

Lanphier, a single man in his early forties, has felt God's call to lay aside his business and become a lay missionary to the city, though he has little training and no formal plan. On the day he launches this ministry—July 1, 1857—his journal contains a few simple statements:

> "Be not weary in well doing."—2 Thess. iii. 13
> "I can do all things through Christ, which strengtheneth me."—Phil. iv. 13.
> Read the fourth chapter 2d Timothy. Think I feel something of the responsibility of the work in which I have engaged. Felt a nearness to God in prayer, and my entire dependence on him from whom cometh all my strength.[7]

A short while later, as Lanphier is out walking, an idea strikes him suddenly, like wet paint flung onto a waiting canvas. His thought is to host a prayer meeting for businessmen. The plan is simple: hold a prayer meeting during the noon hour one day each week, allowing businesspeople to come and go as needed, depending on their schedule.

So he begins.

As advertised, the first noon meeting takes place on Wednesday, September 23, 1857, in a third-story lecture room in a building behind the church. For thirty minutes he prays alone. Then another man ascends the stairs to join him. Then a third. Soon there are six. In Lanphier's words, "The Lord was with us to bless us."

For the second meeting the following Wednesday, twenty are in attendance. The third week, the intercessors number in the thirties. Lanphier determines not to wait another week for the next gathering; they meet the next day and the next, filling a larger room.

Soon the three lecture rooms in the church on Fulton Street cannot hold everyone. More meetings begin in a nearby Methodist church, then in other churches, until thousands are attending.

> . . . the places of prayer multiplied because men were moved to prayer. They wished to pray. They felt impelled, by some unseen power, to pray. They felt the pressure of the call to prayer.[8]

And so it continues, spreading outward through the city. Within six months, ten thousand men and women and children are assembling daily to pray in 150 meeting sites across New York. They sense the earnestness and the love for Christ. Soon the movement spreads to other cities of both north and south, including Boston, Baltimore, Chicago, Cincinnati, Charleston, Memphis, Mobile, New Orleans, Pittsburgh, Savannah, St. Louis, Vicksburg, and Washington. "The whole land received the 'spiritual rain.'"[9]

It all seemed ordained by God in a special way—as observed in a book begun a year after the movement began, to capture the historical facts about it:

> The more we go into the facts of it, the more is the mind filled with adoring wonder and amazement at the stupendous importance and extent of it. Every movement in it seemed to be following, not leading; not creating, but following the developments of a plan already marked out, the end by no means seen from the beginning, and no part of the plan seen, only as it was unfolded, from day to day, by him who devised it all.[10]

In the preface to this work, the author confesses his "awe" at witnessing, "in the midst of this noisy, busy, restless, worldly city," so many solid facts confirming "that the Lord will give his praying people whatsoever they ask in faith!"[11]

These showers of God's favor are what Jonathan Edwards, more than a century earlier, had called *extraordinary prayer*, as he reflected on how God's hand had moved so remarkably in his own community in the 1730s and 1740s, and urgently called for more of such prayer to bring further revival.[12]

ORDINARY PRAYER

But extraordinary prayer isn't the only kind of prayer needed for the awakened urbanite, let alone for the awakening of the urban generation. *Ordinary* prayer—what was once simply called communion with God—is needed as well.

As Dietrich Bonhoeffer put it in *Life Together*, we sometimes "pray for the big things and forget to give thanks for the ordinary, small (and yet really not small) gifts."[13] If extraordinary prayer occurs less often—like a sudden summer thunderstorm ricocheting across the sky—ordinary prayer is morning dew that comes daily, glistening with new life. Ordinary prayer is our *lifestyle* of prayer. A day begins; it begins with prayer.

I love the words of Jeremiah reflecting on the fallen city of Jerusalem, as he remembers God's daily mercy despite heavy chains of sorrow: "His mercies never come to an end; they are new every morning; great is your faithfulness" (Lam. 3:22–23).

Perhaps one of the best resources for learning to pray in and for our cities is the Psalms. Throughout the ages, the book of Psalms has been regarded as the prayer book for God's people, helping cast our gaze toward God's power and beauty.

I've found that starting the day by using the Scriptures, beginning particularly with a Psalm, is an effective way to guide one's prayers, a way to "ignite" one's spiritual life. Martyn Lloyd-Jones once remarked that he reads whatever is necessary in the morning to experience this kind of ignition: "Start by reading something that will warm your spirit. Get rid of a coldness that may have developed in your spirit. You have to learn how to kindle a flame in your spirit, to warm yourself up, to give yourself a start."[14] Lloyd-Jones recommends reading *anything,* but I've found that most consistently the Psalms spark this fire and give shape to ordinary prayer.

They're especially helpful in how they include such a variety of elements: praise, thanksgiving, confession, supplication, lament, intercession. A steady, daily progression through the Psalms brings us an experienced, historic voice. These are *practiced* prayers; they represent, as Annie Dillard says of liturgy, "certain words which people have successfully addressed to God without being killed."[15]

HOW TO PRAY THE PSALMS

The Psalms are intended to be read—and prayed—*existentially.* They're written from existing circumstances (such as David being on the run from Saul, or confessing his adultery). They express an existential condition for the entire community, as well as for the individual reader or pray-er.[16]

Take, for instance, Psalm 51, written after Nathan confronted David for sexual sin. It begins, "Have mercy on me, O God, according to your steadfast love." David quickly brings in vivid imagery: "Blot out my transgressions." He goes on to invoke those familiar words, "Create in me a clean heart, O God, and renew a right spirit within me" (Ps. 51:10). Whose heart is not moved by those words?

In praying the Psalms we remember that they're *poetry*—meant to evoke a mood and stir our senses with the images. Poetry is written to be *felt.* One Bible scholar puts it this way:

> ... the Psalmists make religious and psychological feelings the subject matter of their poetry. Praise, adoration, awe, terror, joy, sorrow, fear, depression—these are what the Psalms are about and therefore lend an emotional aura to them.[17]

As we pray these songs, they connect with us existentially and lift our thoughts up to God. In the urban context, when the mountains are obscured—the psalmist *presents* them (Ps. 36:6; 46:2; 72:3,16); when the "wicked" seem to prevail, the psalmist envisions God *defeating* them (Ps. 1:5; 3:7, 9:5; 75:8).

The Psalms are also meant to be read (and prayed) *historically,* as we're made aware of their original context (easier to determine for some than for others). Many Psalms have a discernible historical situation that rewards our investigation and reflection—by asking, for instance, "Where might David have been when he wrote this?" Or, "How was this Psalm used to call God's people to prayer?"

Especially important is that the Psalms are also meant to be read and prayed in a *Christocentric* way. We move beyond the mere emotion of the Psalm or the historical rootedness of it—to the praise of Christ.

The awakened urbanite prays the Psalms in a Christological way because Christ himself makes it clear that he is the fulfillment of all Old Testament Scripture. After his resurrection, note what Jesus declared to his disciples:

> These are my words that I spoke to you while I was still with you, that *everything written about me* in the Law of Moses and the Prophets *and the Psalms* must be fulfilled. (Luke 24:44)

At this point, the disciples hadn't fully grasped the reality that Jesus fulfilled the Psalms. To enlighten them, Jesus "opened their minds to understand the Scriptures" as he told them this:

> Thus it is written, that the Christ should suffer and on the third day rise from the dead, and that repentance and forgiveness of sins should be proclaimed in his name to all nations, beginning from Jerusalem. You are witnesses of these things. And behold, I am sending the promise of my Father upon you. But stay in the city until you are clothed with power from on high. (24:45–49)

Here he confirms his own personal fulfillment of the Psalms and all the Old Testament.

Even beyond the more obvious messianic Psalms (such as 2, 8, 16, 22, 34, 35, 40, 41, 68, 69, 89, 102, 109, 110, 118), Christ is the embodiment of "the righteous" as mentioned often throughout the Psalms. In the very first Psalm, Jesus is anticipated as the One who "walks not in the counsel of the wicked, nor stands in the way of sinners" (1:1). Only Jesus matches that description perfectly. He, and he alone, is always "like a tree planted by streams of water that yields its fruit in its season" (1:3)—and his fruit is eternal life.

Jesus makes this point with the Pharisees:

> You search the Scriptures because you think that in them you have eternal life; and it is they that *bear witness about me*, yet you refuse to come to me that you may have life. (John 5:39–40)

Thus, as we gladly follow Christ in our urban contexts and seek to re-center our lives on his, and as we learn to pray through the Psalms, there are three points of connection: our praying is existential, historical, and Christocentric.

PRAYING PSALM 22

A brief illustration of this process should help. Take Psalm 22, a famous Psalm quoted many times in the New Testament. This psalm is a lament, a tremendously powerful prayer. Laments generally begin with a *cry* to the Lord and often end, without superficiality, with *confidence* in the Lord.

Psalm 22 begins with a forlorn cry:

> My God, my God, why have you forsaken me?

This is obviously Christological and should be read in this way. (We know this because Jesus uttered these same words on the cross, as we read in Matthew 27:46.)

The psalm concludes with a lengthy triumphant section containing several statements of *confidence*, including these:

> I will tell of your name to my brothers;
> in the midst of the congregation I will praise you. . . .

> From you comes my praise in the great congregation;
> my vows I will perform before those who fear him.
> The afflicted shall eat and be satisfied;
> those who seek him shall praise the LORD!
> May your hearts live forever!

> All the ends of the earth shall remember
> and turn to the LORD,
> and all the families of the nations
> shall worship before you. . . .

they shall come and proclaim his righteousness to a people yet unborn,
   that he has done it. (Ps. 22:22, 25, 26, 27, 31)

The psalmist—and specifically Christ—moves from a cry of desolation to a cry of comfort and consolation. God has forsaken his Son, yet one day there will be a great turning of God's people to himself.

Do you see the change transpiring in the Psalm? Can you see how it helps the soul of the urbanite? Put it this way:

Existentially: It's the experience of every human heart to feel a sense of isolation from the Lord.

Historically: David himself has at various points felt a tremendous sense of abandonment by God, yet he is confident that the Lord will indeed, one day, bring many people to himself.

Christologically: The psalm moves from the sense of abandonment to a sense that God will, and presumably through the mission of the cross (see v. 16 especially), bring a people from the ends of all the earth to himself: "All the ends of the earth shall remember and turn to the LORD" (Ps. 22:27).

So it is that Christ, the crucified and risen One who is Lord of all, and Lord of the city, should be central to our lives in prayer.

FURTHER SUGGESTIONS

I encourage you to grow in prayer, particularly in praying according to the Psalms, but also to pray prayers of big faith—individually and corporately—for God to work in our cities and in our lives. If we're to follow God radically and faithfully in the city, if we're to see ourselves and our cities awakened in the urban generation, then positioning Christ as central to our prayer lives is critical.

Let me conclude this chapter by summarizing practical suggestions for praying urbanites:

1. Again, *use the Psalms to start the day*.

2. *Use a Bible reading plan if possible.* There are many excellent lectionary reading plans available. I like the plan developed in the 1800s by Robert Murray McCheyne (available in several online sites) as well as the *ESV Study Bible* reading plan, as both lead you through the whole of the Bible but have an emphasis on the Psalms.

3. *Pray in community and individually.* If you're married, start the day in prayer with your spouse. If you're single, a brief prayer to begin the day with a roommate or a coworker can be beneficial.

4. *Pray spiritually.* That is, pray in the power of the Spirit. Prayer lists are good—lists of people to pray for and requests to bring up—but they're not required. If you're a list person, all the better for you. If you're *not,* then pray for people as they come to mind. If you've said you'll pray for someone, do pray for them.

5. *Pray for our cities.* Even as Abraham spoke to God earnestly about the salvation of Sodom, let's give ourselves as well to prayer for our cities, pointing to Christ as the Righteous One.

Praying is not, of course, specifically urban. But the urbanite needs daily the awakening of prayer and of the Psalms. We need to pray; we were made to pray; we were made for communion with God.

A CLOSING PRAYER

Our Father in heaven,

Holy is your name. We approach you humbly today in prayer. Like Abraham, we are "but dust and ashes." Yet we also come before you boldly because of your Son—to ask for the salvation of our cities. Like Abraham, we pray with courage—surrendering to your will.

Bring another day, O Lord, as you have in the past, when many, many in our city and throughout the world return to you, when cities are filled with prayer, repentance, forgiveness, new life in Christ—and adoring wonder and amazement at your glory.

We know that no one is truly righteous other than your Son; we know that our cities, because of our sin and your holiness, deserve destruction, including us. But we look to Christ, our Savior, and ask you to save some, even many.

We pray for ourselves, our neighbors, our family, and our colleagues. Move men and women to pray. Spread this movement of prayer to cities north and south, east and west, until "in the midst of our noisy, busy, restless, worldly cities" we see that it is your hand that has devised it all.

In the name of Christ,

Amen.

4

THE CITY TRANSFORMED

Fields and trees are not willing to teach me anything;
but this can be effected by men residing in the city.

PLATO

The voice of the LORD cries to the city—
and it is sound wisdom to fear your name:
"Hear of the rod and of him who appointed it!"

MICAH 6:9

We've been asking in these opening chapters, *What does God think of cities?* Some people, we know, look at cities in a strongly negative way, while others have quite idealistic views. But what is *God's* view?

As we look at various Scriptures from Genesis to Revelation related to this topic, we want to know what it means to be a twenty-first century urbanite rooted in the city but who is also trying to serve and love God. What does it mean to be fully involved in a city when your mind and heart are saturated with the Scriptures, and you seek to exalt Jesus and lift up his name?

And in that pursuit, can we truly know a life of peace and joy in the city? After all, cities everywhere are famous for blights—like the reputation for political corruption in my hometown, Chicago. Various cities are renowned for greed, grime, rudeness, violence, economic oppression, superficiality, substance abuse, sexual depravity, or other undesirable traits. Do we somehow have to compromise with such things to be a real part of the city?

WHO'S ANGRY?

Anger is another frequent urban trait, and one that some experts say is on the rise—especially road rage on urban thoroughfares and highways. Road rage is increasing, psychiatrists say, because of today's persistent and wide-spread economic stress. But even without our economic woes, driving in congested urban traffic can easily induce anger, according to Dr. Charles Raison, a psychiatrist at Emory University. He says road rage is "pervasive, especially in the biggest cities. . . . Other drivers become faceless, anonymous objects. We know from research that this plays into this evolved human tendency to be meaner, more hostile. We are just ruder in cars, more prickly toward strangers. Road rage is a way to pass off your misery."[1]

In a startling way, *anger* also shows up in one of the most urban-focused books of the Bible.

It's the book of Jonah, one of the Bible's most famous stories—action-packed, fast-paced, tightly constructed, and crammed full of shocks and surprises. In this brief account of a prophet on the run from God, Jonah's anger becomes a magnifying glass, giving us a close-up perspective not only on Jonah himself, but also on God's view of cities.

The close of the story demonstrates something that's true about us all: the things we get angry about often expose what we really value, and how we expect the world to work. It also reveals ultimately what we think about God.

Near the end of the story is where we suddenly see Jonah's anger exploding. God had shown amazing compassion toward the wicked and violent city of Nineveh, choosing not to destroy it after the people miraculously turned to God in one of the swiftest and greatest revivals in history. The city is literally transformed by God's grace. Now that's amazing and wonderful, right? But here's how God's prophet reacted: "It displeased Jonah exceedingly, and *he was angry*" (Jonah 4:1). One Bible scholar translates it this way: "Jonah was deeply offended and furious."[2]

But *why?*

A fast trip back through this story, for a closer look, will help us find the answer and how it relates to us today.

GO TO THE GREAT CITY

The story begins with an urban call:

> Now the word of the LORD came to Jonah . . . "Arise, *go to Nineveh, that great city,* and call out against it, for their evil has come up before me." (Jonah 1:1–2)

That great city[3]—like so many cities in our day. Jonah wouldn't need to be told about Nineveh's greatness, but God wanted to emphasize this fact—both for his prophet's sake and for all who read his story, including you and me.

Nineveh was indeed the leading city in the Assyrian empire, the world's superpower of that day, feared by all its neighbors. An additional reason for Nineveh's renown was simply its longevity. It was one of the world's oldest cities, perhaps even *the* oldest. It's mentioned in Genesis 10:8–12 (along with Shinar and Babel) as being founded by Noah's descendant Nimrod. But the biggest fame-factor for Nineveh was simply its status as the nerve center of a brutal, bloodthirsty nation. Nobody called Nineveh a nice place.

The Assyrians cultivated an aura of arrogant viciousness, featuring "deliberate terror and atrocity as instruments of public policy."[4] A century before Jonah's time, one Assyrian king boasted of one of his military campaigns with these words:

> I caused great slaughter. . . . I destroyed, I demolished, I burned. I took their warriors prisoner and impaled them on stakes before their cities.

He goes on to describe a battle where thousands were killed and numerous others imprisoned:

> Many of the captives I burned in a fire. Many I took alive; from some I cut off their hands to the wrist, from others I cut off their noses, ears, and fingers; I put out the eyes of many of the soldiers. I burnt their young men and women to death.[5]

This same cruel king (Ashurnasirpal II) recorded in writing how he had skinned alive "many nobles who had rebelled against me"; he then had their skins either piled up, or "erected on stakes upon the pile," or "draped . . . over the walls" of Nineveh. This gory king concludes, "Thus have I constantly established my victory and strength over the land."[6]

Such was the heritage and reputation of Nineveh and Assyria. "Ninevite values are the opposite of Israelite values,"[7] concludes one scholarly observer, who then gives a good description of the city's strange and imposing blend of grandeur and barbarity, especially as it affected the people of God:

> King Sennacherib . . . launched an impressive building program and constructed a magnificent city, extending and beautifying Nineveh to become the showplace of its day, a veritable ancient Versailles with a palace, temple, gardens, and administrative buildings. From the capital city, wars were launched, and the Ninevites established a reputation for brutality. . . .
>
> The Jews would not have forgotten the humiliation and ill treatment they received at the hands of Nineveh's leaders and citizens. The Assyrians invaded surrounding territory repeatedly as they burned and plundered cities and deported the inhabitants. To the Israelites, the immorality and criminality of Nineveh would be self-evident, and they would have good reason to continue fearing Ninevite rapine. The town is associated with political deceit, military savagery, violent plunder, and blasphemous anti-God practices.[8]

But more important about Nineveh than such historical details is the simple fact stated by God to his prophet Jonah: "their evil has come up *before me*" (Jonah 1:2). In God's eyes, the people of Nineveh stood condemned for their wicked ways.

Understandably, Jonah would scarcely be inclined to look upon this city with any fondness.

It helps here to know more of this prophet's background. Jonah was apparently a country boy. In 2 Kings 14:25 we learn that he was from "Gath-hepher," a location in Galilee just three miles from the site of Nazareth, where the boy Jesus would mature into manhood eight centuries later. Jonah would be more at home on Galilee's green hillsides than in some teeming urban center like Nineveh.

Moreover, Jonah had become famous among his countrymen even before the book of Jonah opens. That same passage in 2 Kings tells us that as the Lord's "servant," Jonah prophesied an expansion and strengthening of Israel's northern border, which was indeed accomplished in the reign of King Jeroboam II. This was the border facing toward the dangerous, oppressive, ever-expanding Assyrian empire. Jonah's encouraging word came at a time when "the LORD saw that the affliction of Israel was very bitter, for . . . there was none to help Israel" (2 Kings 14:26). Nineveh and Assyria were no doubt the source of Israel's bitter affliction. But in this dark hour, Jonah's word brought light and inspiration, enabling Israel to fortify herself despite her lack of resources.

This was the man whom God assigned to go to great Nineveh and prophesy against it.

HURLED ABOUT

From the famous story that unfolds, we know how Jonah immediately responds. Almost laughably, he heads in the opposite direction, trying to "flee . . . from the presence of the LORD" (Jonah 1:3). He buys passage on a boat to Tarshish—most likely the city by that name on the Mediterranean's far western shore, about as far as one could get from Nineveh in the then-known world.

But of course the voyage is interrupted when a massive Mediterranean storm arises from a "great wind" that God "hurled" (1:4) from on high. The pagan sailors discover (from Jonah's own words) that he's dodging God, and they confront him. Cornered, Jonah tells them to "hurl" him into the sea—for he realizes that these men will otherwise drown with him on the doomed ship. The sailors are unwilling to cast him overboard, but the storm only worsens. Eventually, after praying to the Lord, they toss him over, which immediately causes the storm to be stilled. The sailors, recognizing God at work and overwhelmingly affected by it, offer him a sacrifice.

Meanwhile Jonah becomes one of history's most famous meals, all because "the LORD *appointed* a great fish to swallow up Jonah" (1:17). Enduring an unimaginably traumatic experience inside the fish's belly for "three days and three nights," Jonah prays with intensity and even eloquence. "And the LORD spoke to the fish, and it vomited Jonah out upon the dry land" (2:10).

Standing at last on dry ground, with a fresh start in life, Jonah is divinely recommissioned as if nothing had happened:

> Then the word of the LORD came to Jonah the second time, saying, "Arise, *go to Nineveh, that great city,* and call out against it the message that I tell you." (3:1–2)

God has a purpose for this prophet, and he won't be thwarted, even by the prophet's own failures and resistance.

The text immediately puts even more stress on Nineveh's greatness. As Jonah finally obeys and travels toward Nineveh, we're told that "Nineveh was *an exceedingly great city*, three days' journey in breadth" (3:3). Not just great, but "exceedingly great." This city is vastly significant in population and power but also in sheer size (and surely in other ways, too, in the mind of God). A literal translation of the Hebrew is that Nineveh was "a great city to God." All this again reminds us of many a metropolis spread throughout our own world today.

Jonah heads toward Nineveh's city center and calls out the blunt and terrible message God has given him: "Yet forty days, and Nineveh shall be overthrown!" (3:4). We know from later on (v. 10) that this isn't merely a message Jonah made up; it is indeed God's word to this people in this moment. God's concern for the people of this city is that they hear his word.

A CITY'S SALVATION

The people's response to this stranger strikes us as being nothing short of absolutely incredible:

> And the people of Nineveh *believed God*. They called for a fast and put on sackcloth, from the greatest of them to the least of them. (Jonah 3:5)

We go on to read how even the king "arose from his throne, removed his robe, covered himself with sackcloth, and sat in ashes." He decrees a fast not only for all the people, but for their livestock as well. And he orders the people to pray: "let them call out mightily to God." His words acknowledge Nineveh's universal guilt: "Let *everyone* turn from his evil way and from the violence that is in his hands" (3:6–8).

For king and commoner alike, in every neighborhood and in all the social strata, the eyes of people's hearts are opened to see the truth of their spiritual need. They understand they have no other choice but to look to the Lord and seek the deliverance he alone can bring. So they commit to doing nothing else except plead with him. As the king expresses it, "Who knows? God may turn and relent and turn from his fierce anger, so that we may not perish" (3:9). Praying is no guarantee—but God's mercy is their only hope.

And their prayers are answered:

When God saw what they did, how they turned from their evil way, God relented of the disaster that he had said he would do to them, and he did not do it. (3:10)

But note here how *proclamation* is key. Without the proclamation in Nineveh of God's word—even from such a flawed and unlikely messenger—the city's spiritual turnaround would never have occurred. "The people of Nineveh *believed God*" (Jonah 3:5); they recognized *God's* authority behind even such a stark and unattractive message as the one Jonah gave them.

It's a reminder to us: even in this era of gospel grace, *preaching* is the catalyst for personal and widespread city-change. No city or citizen will ever experience pervasive change without effective gospel proclamation—the intentional announcing of the character, love, wrath, and holiness of the living God. This is the hope of our cities.

As we see in Jonah, the greatest need of the city is the greatest news of all. Paul urgently asks, "And how are they to hear without someone *preaching*? And how are they to preach unless they are sent? As it is written, 'How beautiful are the feet of those who preach the good news!'" (Rom. 10:14–15). Jonah's rebellious feet are beautiful.

Kneeling in sackcloth and ashes, crying out to God, the king and people of Nineveh had this hope: "that we may not *perish*" (Jonah 3:9). They understood that they indeed were destined to perish—but they turned from their sins to seek desperately for divine deliverance. In Jesus, our cities today have the Savior who fills this exact need for them, as the gospel makes so abundantly clear: "For God so loved the world, that he gave his only Son, that whoever believes in him *should not perish* but have eternal life" (John 3:16). Thus, in such an unlikely place as the story of Jonah, we find a call to a theology of preaching the gospel in all its saving power.

The central message of Jonah is found in his prayer in the belly of the fish: "Salvation belongs to the LORD" (Jonah 2:9). God is the author of salvation, and to communicate his mercy he uses even imperfect, disobedient people—people who run the wrong way. God has ordained that salvation comes through the proclamation of his saints. In this urban generation, our vast cities need the greatest news of all—the message of Jesus' life-giving death and resurrection.

ANGER FLASH

And now we're back to the point in that story where Jonah's anger enters in. He has observed an entire city repent from sin and turn to God, by faith, for salvation. He has seen the glory of God's mercy as he withheld destruction that was well deserved. Yet this miracle drives Jonah into a rage-inspired depression.

Listen carefully to his words, as Jonah vents:

> O Lord, is not this what I said when I was yet in my country? That is why I made haste to flee to Tarshish; for I knew that you are a gracious God and merciful, slow to anger and abounding in steadfast love, and relenting from disaster. Therefore now, O Lord, please take my life from me, for it is better for me to die than to live. (Jonah 4:2–3)

Jonah can quote Scripture aplenty about God's love and mercy and slowness to anger, but he obviously doesn't really *get* it. He would rather watch the Ninevites get obliterated than see them revitalized by God's mercy.

This prophet knows just enough of the Lord's character, and just enough of the Scriptures, to realize that the divine message of judgment toward Nineveh was in fact *designed* to produce repentance and an opportunity to receive divine mercy. That's why Jonah fled God's presence in the first place—he wanted no part of making such an opportunity possible for Nineveh.

As Jonah was tramping through Nineveh's crowded streets blurting out his message from God, his heart must have *still* been so hardened that not a single face in those multitudes evoked his pity or sparked any empathy—even when these people were so obviously gripped by his message. For Jonah, they're just nameless, faceless people.

You know what it can be like in a crowded urban scene, on a subway or at a festival—people are pressed around you, yet you don't really know them or connect with them. They're nothing more than part of the landscape, and it's so easy to move toward apathy or even judgmentalism—which is exactly the turn Jonah takes. Jonah observes these people in the massive crowd, but he can't truly *see* any of them. He's essentially blind.

But not God. "God *saw* what they did" (Jonah 3:10). And seeing their repentance moves him to mercy.

When we, too, rightly see the masses of the city, when we start to view them from God's perspective, we also begin to sense his gracious and loving heart toward them. We see them as Christ did—as when he looked at the city and wept (Luke 19:41).

SLOW ANGER, PERFECT PATIENCE

Our picture of that grace and love in God's heart only intensifies as the story of Jonah rapidly concludes.

Jonah had said to God, "I knew that you are a gracious God and merciful, *slow to anger*" (Jonah 4:2). It's not that God is *never* angry—though many modern people don't like the idea that he ever would be. We can have a hard time dealing with Scriptures that speak of his anger, that clearly tell of a coming day of judgment when God's wrath is revealed (for example, Rom. 2:5 or 2 Thess. 1:6–10). But the truth is there. Yes, he is a God of wrath. Yet he's also *slow* to anger, as Scripture equally insists (Ex. 34:6–7; Ps. 86:15; 145:8).

It's because the God of wrath is slow to anger that he doesn't go ahead and torch Nineveh (no matter how much his servant Jonah wants to see divine fireworks) but gives her people ample opportunity for repentance. And he richly provides the same opportunities in all our cities today. "The Lord . . . is patient toward you, not wishing that any should perish, but that all should reach repentance" (2 Pet. 3:9).

Jonah's indignant attitude only heightens by contrast the attitude of God. Watching Nineveh get its reprieve, Jonah tells God that he's so angry about it he could die (Jonah 4:3). God could easily arrange for that, but he's showing mercy and patience to Jonah as well. He asks his prophet, "Do you do well to be angry?" (4:4); he wants Jonah to measure and weigh this anger, to determine if it's really justified. It's a good question to ask ourselves too, whenever our anger is on the rise. *What is my anger revealing about my heart, my misdirected desires, my unreasonable expectations? Where am I disconnected from God's patience and love? How am I failing to view myself and my neighbors as God views them?*

Next for Jonah comes a brief and surprising episode that further reveals God's heart and Jonah's narrowness. Jonah had gone beyond the outskirts of Nineveh, out in the desert, and he had fashioned a little shelter for shade. There he stationed himself "till he should see what would become of the city" (4:5).

God graciously caused a large plant to suddenly sprout beside Jonah and spread upward—"that it might be a shade over his head, to save him from his discomfort" (4:6). The text says that the Lord "appointed" this plant—the same Hebrew word as used earlier when the Lord "appointed a great fish to swallow up Jonah" (1:17). Divine sovereignty is being emphasized; God is in control. In all things, from the largest matters of salvation for a whole city to even the private details of one man's relief from suffering, God is in charge. Then and now, all our comforts come ultimately from the Lord's hand alone.

Not surprisingly, "Jonah was exceedingly glad because of the plant" (4:6). He is now as extremely pleased with this comfort as he had been "exceedingly" displeased over Nineveh's pardon from God (4:1).

But the welcomed plant is taken away as quickly as it had sprung up. The following morning, "God appointed [there's that word again] a worm that attacked the plant, so that it withered"; moments later, "God appointed a scorching east wind, and the sun beat down on the head of Jonah so that he was faint" (4:7–8).

This triggers further conversation between God and Jonah, straight from their hearts. Jonah announces once more he wants to die; God ignores this request and instead calls again for Jonah's heart assessment: "Do you do well to be angry for the plant?" Jonah is insistent: "Yes, I do well to be angry, angry enough to die" (4:9).

The anger in his hardened heart is revealing Jonah's idolatry. He loves the plant more than the people—more even than God's mercy! It has been said that idolatry is when a good thing (like a career, a family, a home, a relationship—even a shade tree) becomes an ultimate thing, an "everything." God himself had provided the plant; but Jonah's heart is clutched around it, so that when it is taken away, he is plunged from extreme pleasure to the depths of depression.

It's a moment that vividly exposes Jonah's idol of comfort, his idol of self-interest, his idol of self-protection—as well as his unwillingness to participate in God's mission.

Part of what we're intended to see in Jonah is our own idolatries—our own need for God's grace. When do *we* run from God? What aspects of God's mission do *we* overlook for our priorities and even our comforts? In what ways are *our* hearts numbed as we encounter a city and see it merely as a mass of people?

THE RIGHT COMPASSION, THE RIGHT REASONS

God gets the last word in Jonah's story. "You pity the plant," he says, "for which you did not labor, nor did you make it grow, which came into being in a night and perished in a night" (Jonah 4:10). The word for "pity" carries the idea of compassion, of giving relief, of seeking the other's welfare. For the time being, God is overlooking Jonah's idolatrous self-interest; for the sake of discussion, he assumes his prophet's genuine consideration for the plant's well-being.

Then the Lord goes on to make his real point, drawing the attention to himself as he asks, "And should not I pity Nineveh, *that great city*, in which there are more than 120,000 persons who do not know their right hand from their left, and also much cattle?" (4:11).

The phrase about not knowing the right hand from the left hand is an ancient one that often refers to moral and spiritual blindness and ignorance—a condition that always seemed entrenched in Nineveh. Meanwhile the added phrase, "and also much cattle," reminds us that *all* life would have perished under God's announced destruction of Nineveh. This was something the Assyrian king seemed to recognize when he announced a citywide fast, calling even for herds and flocks to be deprived of food and water, so their bellowing might be joined to the loud cries of Ninevites seeking God's mercy.

Just think of the huge contrast between Jonah's "pity" and God's. Jonah's concern is microscopic; God's is macroscopic. Jonah sees a close-by vine that brings him personal comfort, and his heart breaks when it's gone. But the Lord God sees *that great city*—and has great compassion for it. God's word comes to a city, and the result is miraculous life and renewal for thousands upon thousands.

This chapter is intended to help us examine our hearts. God wants us to study our prejudices, our priorities, our tendency to hardness of heart, and bring all this before him. He wants us to see that salvation belongs to him, and that he chooses to use proclamation to save a city, even through imperfect people.

Like Nineveh of old, our urban generation needs a Savior, and his name is Jesus. There "is no other name under heaven given among men by which we must be saved" (Acts 4:12). Not everyone is called to take the gospel to a city, but we should see what Jonah did not see: cities matter to God. A city is people, people made in God's image yet cut off from him. All of us who see his grace and mercy should respond by supporting the essential necessity of the proclamation of God's Word in our cities.

We need a movement of the gospel in our cities. We need the global church today to engage the cities of the world with a massive understanding and living out of the gospel. *Should we not be concerned,* God asks, *about these cities?* For God cares deeply for the masses of the city.

And yes, we also need a movement of the gospel to every corner of the earth. Both are necessary. People matter to him, because they're eternal. But cities are filled with people. *God loves people* in all their diversity, in all their need.

Here's an exercise. Take a walk through a city near you—and try seeing the people there as God looks at them. Pray for them as you acknowledge his heart: "Yes, Lord, you love them; yes, of course, you *should* love them and care for them, and I know you do. Show me and teach me this love."

Jesus has promised that the people who walked the streets of Nineveh in Jonah's day are people we'll hear from again. He tells us that we'll one day look upon the faces of the Ninevites—no longer nameless or faceless—and that they'll magnify the importance of Jesus Christ. He promises in Matthew 12:41 that the Ninevites "will rise up at the judgment" and condemn the generation that rejects him. Why? Because Nineveh's people "repented at the preaching of Jonah, and behold, *something greater than Jonah is here."*

This final Prophet has come, One far greater and better than Jonah. He's the Prophet who doesn't run away from God, but willingly walks to his own death. He is thrown overboard into the grave to save us from the storms of God's wrath. He completely carries out the Father's will in every way—he who "humbled himself by becoming obedient to the point of death, even death on a cross" (Phil. 2:8). Jesus is the Prophet who loves the masses more than he loves his own comfort, and who therefore "emptied himself, by taking the form of a servant" (2:7), and securing the eternal comfort of all in every city who will believe. "Take my life away," he says, "but give life to the masses."

Jonah had gone outside the city to seek his comfort and nurse his personal anger; in contrast, Jesus went outside the city to yield to the anger of his crucifiers. Nailed to the cross, he bore the wrath of God for the sins of mankind—for all who repent, urban and non-urban. Thus he proved forever, for you and me, the vastness of God's pity and love for "that great city" . . . and for every great city.

God's grace is greater than any city, greater than all our anger, greater than all our running away. This urban generation needs the awakening we see in the book of Jonah. Our cities need the enlivening of *this* gospel.

A CLOSING PRAYER

Father,

Thank you for your Word. When we look at Jonah—and his petty desires—it exposes our own love for comfort, our own anger, our own idolatries and prejudices. Our hearts are not always soft to those around us, to our neighbors, to our colleagues, to those who need you. Most of all, O Lord, our hearts are not always soft to you.

But you, O God of infinite justice, are also a God of mercy; you are moved with compassion for the scores of people who are nameless to us; you are willing to pursue even those who have run from you. Salvation, O Lord, is in your hands. Salvation belongs to you. Save us, O Lord, save our cities. Let our voices come to you in your holy temple.

We thank you for Jesus, who intentionally threw himself into the jaws of death that we might live. We praise you with our voice of thanksgiving.

In the name of Jesus,
Amen.

5

FAITHFULNESS IN THE CITY

I had an architectonic vision of what a city might be . . .
a city planned, built, and conducted as a community enterprise. . . .
I saw cities as social agencies that would make life easier for people,
full of pleasure, beauty, and opportunity.

FREDERIC HOWE, *THE CONFESSIONS OF A REFORMER*

They were strangers and exiles on the earth.

HEBREWS 11:13

I've been captivated by a certain book written more than a century ago, a classic and fascinating work for anyone interested in the rise of urbanization and people's response to it.

Titled simply *Plan of Chicago*, it was written in the opening decade of the 1900s by Daniel H. Burnham and Edward H. Bennett (both were architects and city planners), with backing from the Commercial Club of Chicago. Unlike anything ever seen before, its appearance represents a "signal moment in the history of the American city"; it has been called "a plan that reshaped American notions of the modern city."[1] *Plan of Chicago* blazed a trail in the emerging field of city planning, and is said in fact to have "revolutionized urban design."[2]

THINK FUTURE, THINK BIG

On the opening page of this innovative work, Daniel Burnham acknowledges the growing fact of modern urbanization—along with a shared and natural desire to better control its quality and direction: "the time has come to bring order out of the chaos. . . . a plan for a well-ordered and convenient city is seen to be indispensable."[3]

To bring about such order and convenience, Burnham and Bennett's wide-ranging and beautifully illustrated book envisioned expanded parks on Chicago's lakeshore and throughout the city, wider and more systematically arranged streets (including numerous diagonal arteries dramatically interrupting the standard squarish grid), improved public transportation terminals, and new cultural centers and other public places.

This book represented "the last creative public work undertaken by Mr. Burnham," who "regarded it as the supreme effort of his life"; fittingly, his plan was praised not only for its comprehensiveness but also for "its physical and spiritual content, the unlimited and enduring qualities which project it into an indefinite future."[4] His vision stretched forward multiple decades. Many of his detailed, far-reaching proposals have indeed been carried out in Chicago over the past century, and in various ways his plan continues to inspire and impact the city's development.

Meanwhile, for urban planners and thinkers everywhere, Burnham's overall planning philosophy in *Plan of Chicago* still exemplifies a full-picture approach with long-term vision. "The *Plan*'s most important heritage is the persistence of the idea that it is necessary to think not only big but also comprehensively."[5]

As a strategy for a city's physical and aesthetic transformation, Burnham's work is exemplary. But the very existence of his magisterial work raises an important question: what about a plan for a city's *spiritual* transformation—a plan for *renewal* that impacts a city culturally, physically, and spiritually?

Should not the wandering urbanite as well as the devoted follower of Jesus be concerned not merely with new parks and roads—but with something deeper?

GOD'S URBAN PLAN

When thinking about God's plans for them, here's a favorite verse for many:

> For I know the plans I have for you, declares the LORD, plans for welfare and not for evil, to give you a future and a hope. (Jer. 29:11)

The encouragement to be found in this passage is profound. The word translated here as "welfare" is *shalom*—the Hebrew term for wholeness and completeness, and for peaceful well-being. It's easy to see why many hearts welcome such a promise so warmly.

But modern readers often overlook its context. The verse isn't written to individuals. This is part of a letter sent to God's people living in urban exile in faraway Babylon. Its message is a surprising one—still today offering wisdom and practical guidance to the souls of all God's people no matter where they live—but particularly those in difficult urban settings.

Seen in context, this favorite passage offers a simple but robust approach to long-term faithfulness in the city.

Near the beginning of the sixth century BC, the Jews to whom Jeremiah wrote this letter found themselves in the imposing pagan city of Babylon because of a series of forced relocations. Their enemy, the mighty Babylonians, would later perpetrate further aggressions against the Jews, leading in time to the complete destruction of Jerusalem, the cessation of the Jewish homeland in Palestine, and a further and much greater relocation of God's people in Babylon. So the displaced Jews already captive in Babylon were the vanguard of many more to come.

God, in his wise concern, directed his prophet Jeremiah to send them a message that was greatly needed. Here they were, trapped in a locale where they didn't fit in, where customs, laws, foods, language, and ways of life were all so strangely different. They lived in one place, while longing deeply and inescapably for another. *If somehow we could only get back home! How long, O Lord?*

Our link, as followers of Christ, to these exiles in Babylon is perhaps stronger than we might imagine. The book of Hebrews reminds us of a certain mind-set prevailing among God's saints across the generations—how they "acknowledged that they were strangers and exiles on the earth" (Heb. 11:13). "I am a sojourner on the earth," the psalmist had confessed (Ps. 119:19), and the apostle Peter agrees—he addresses believers in Christ as "sojourners and exiles" and speaks of earthly life as "the time of your exile" (1 Pet. 2:11; see also 1:17).

No matter where you live, no matter how comfortable or chaotic the conditions, if you're a Christian you're displaced from your eternal home where you really belong. It brings a certain sense of homesickness, something C. S. Lewis described as "the stab, the pang, the inconsolable longing."[6] It's a yearning that will be with you wherever you wander in this world, something you'll feel wherever God has placed you. It's not because you belong out in the wilderness, or even in some different city; it's because "our citizenship is in heaven, and from it we await a Savior, the Lord Jesus Christ" (Phil. 3:20).

The Jewish exiles addressed by Jeremiah would sense deeply that they were not citizens of Babylon. But in that regard, the prophet's letter would include some startling details.

A PRACTICAL MESSAGE OF GOD'S CONCERN

Imagine the scene in Babylon among these exiles as news spread of a letter's arrival from their beloved homeland. I picture God's people streaming out their doorways, gathering excitedly to hear the words read aloud.

Here was far more than just news from back home. This letter from Jeremiah, the Lord's prophet, carried a personal word *straight from God* for these resident aliens in an oppressive environment.

That message began:

> Thus says the LORD of hosts, the God of Israel, to all the exiles whom I have sent into exile from Jerusalem to Babylon. (Jer. 29:4)

There's encouragement for them here, right from the start. Notice the strong assertion not only of divine authorship but also of divine sovereignty. God is reminding them, "You're in Babylon because of *me*—I'm the One who placed you there." He wanted them to see his hand behind their relocation. And the very existence of this letter was a demonstration of God's continuing care for them in their place of captivity. (In their case, such encouragement was no doubt particularly welcome since their displacement was due to God's discipline for their persistent disobedience in the past.)

As the people heard those opening words from their sovereign Lord, they could well wonder: *What will he have to say to us? What concern will God show us, what encouragement, what guidance? Will he communicate mercy, and extend a promise of our quick return home?*

They would listen breathlessly. And the essence of this letter's message, they would quickly discover, is that God wanted his people to put down roots in their new urban setting, and to thrive there.

That message comes through memorably in a series of paired imperatives, very practical in nature:

Thus says the LORD of hosts . . .

Build houses and live in them;
plant gardens and eat their produce.

Take wives and have sons and daughters;
take wives for your sons, and give your daughters in marriage,

that they may bear sons and daughters;
multiply there, and do not decrease. (Jer. 29:4–6)

These words would cut immediately to the core issue for God's people in exile, which was this: *How long must this hostile city be our home? How long, O Lord, are we to dwell here?*

FALSE HOPES

In their case, this hard question of *how long* was being intensified through the actions of certain troublemakers. As if the exiles' natural longing for home wasn't already strong enough, false prophets were fanning the flames of the people's desire for returning to their homeland. The story of one of these deceivers, named Hananiah, is highlighted in the previous chapter of Jeremiah.

Hananiah had marched into Jerusalem's temple and "in the presence of the priests and all the people" confronted Jeremiah with some bold assertions. In only two years, he announced, God would "break the yoke" of Babylon's King Nebuchadnezzar and bring all those Jewish exiles back home. "Thus says the LORD of hosts," Hananiah audaciously declared (Jer. 28:1–4).

Jeremiah had stood up to this rival prophet and countered those claims: "Listen, Hananiah, the LORD has not sent you, and you have made this people trust in a lie" (28:15). Hananiah's deception was evil, Jeremiah declared, and his punishment would be severe: "Therefore thus says the LORD: 'Behold, I will remove you from the face of the earth. This year you shall die, because you have uttered rebellion against the LORD'" (28:16).

True to Jeremiah's word, Hananiah died a short while later—but by then, the potent false prophecy most likely had made its way to the captives in Babylon. Mingled with the lies of other false prophets in Babylon who were active among the exiles (as seen in 29:20–32), it must have stirred up their expectations for a getaway just around the corner. Understandably, they would eagerly embrace any prediction of a short exile.

INVESTING IN THIS PAGAN CITY

But in Jeremiah's letter, those false hopes would be squarely confronted with God's higher counsel: "Build . . . plant . . . marry . . . multiply . . ." (Jer. 29:5–6). In essence the Lord was telling them, *"Don't put your life on hold* just because you'd prefer being somewhere else. Your being in this place is *my plan.* So invest in this city where I've sent you; make the most of it—build community, build relationships, build families."

God gave them this message asking for long-term commitment to Babylon even though he also prophesied at length that Babylon eventually would be destroyed (Isaiah 13–14; 21; 47; Jeremiah 50–51; Habakkuk 2). Nevertheless his plan was for his people to make this communal investment in Babylon—among *the very people who had oppressed them*—for no less than seventy years (as we'll see).

Call it God's Babylonian plan for *shalom.* This commitment was true first in a *residential sense* ("build houses and live in them"; Jer. 29:5). For now, this was *home,* as fully reflected in the physical realities of housing and shelter. But more than just sufficient housing, cities need residents who make a long-term, radical, communal investment there. Our cities are filled with wandering urbanites, and if we, like them, are just passing through, there's a tendency to think, "I'll just get what I can out of this city, use it for what I need and then move on." We become consumers, not contributors. That's not what God calls his people to do. They invest!

The commitment God called for was true also in the areas of *vocation and sustenance* ("plant gardens and eat their produce"; v. 5)—making a contribution to the economy. They were to *plant* something in the city.

This may seem incidental, but gardens have a tendency to humanize and slow down our culture. Think of how, on a larger scale, Central Park has shaped Manhattan, or of how the trees and grass and open space in your local park give a sense of peacefulness. Our cities, approached carelessly, are filled with trash, debris, and graffiti; they need intentional cultivation and tending. Some days I can literally pick up a full bag of garbage in my front yard, just from passersby. But a "cultivation mindset" that actively plants within the city inherently works against flippant urban consumerism.

There's even the hint, a tiny seed, of something deeper here—the doctrine of vocation. This concept looks back at God's intentions for work—at Adam as gardener—and values what we *do* with our lives. Even the simple things. This concept is rooted in God's sovereignty. As Abraham Kuyper famously put it, "There is not one square inch of the entire creation about which Jesus Christ does not cry out, 'This is mine! This belongs to me!'"[7] This was true also of Babylon. Yahweh was as sovereign over Babylon as Christ is today over Bogotá or Dallas; over Eugene, Oregon; or Broken Arrow, Oklahoma.

This wholehearted investment was also to be demonstrated through *family, community and multi-generational family growth* ("Take wives and have sons and daughters; take wives for your sons, and give your daughters in marriage, that they may bear sons and daughters"; Jer. 29:6). God's people in oppressive Babylon were to build long-term *relational* structures as well as the *physical* structures mentioned earlier.

Notice that Jeremiah challenges God's people to think about *three generations* of faithfulness. They're not merely to marry and have children, but also to *raise* their children in Babylon so that *they also* may have children. They were to think not just about the present generation and the next, but also about the generations beyond—that's the biblical perspective.

The psalmist Asaph impresses this same generational perspective, reminding Israel that God's law was something "which he commanded our fathers to teach to their children, that the next generation might know them, the children yet unborn, and arise and tell them to their children, so that they should set their hope in God and not forget the works of God" (Ps. 78:5–7). In today's cities, families often move out once their children reach school age. Jeremiah's charge reverses that trend for the good and welfare of the city. Our cities need a long-term communal presence.

Taken all together—this vision for *residential, vocational, relational,* and *generational* commitments adds up to one reality—a radical, God-fearing, multiplying community. God's people here are to "multiply . . . and do not decrease." Cultivating this long-term mind-set of investment means recognizing that our cities need godly influence in *every* realm, including business, law, education, government, the arts, and more.

From a New Testament perspective, our cities need the overall increase of those who love and follow Christ. Yet in many of our most influential cities, the gospel-believing population has declined to less than one percent (that's the figure for Paris, for example). Jeremiah's vision calls for a reversal of that trend, even in an oppressive environment.

LONG TERM RESOLVE

Long-term, residential commitment takes radical resolve.

Civil rights activist and author John Perkins was nearly killed by racist police who beat him within an inch of death and choked him by stuffing a fork down his throat.[8] But he was radically changed by God's love to seek the long-term welfare of his city, Jackson, Mississippi.

Perkins has written a number of books and helped start a movement called Christian Community Development Association, which restores broken urban communities. One of the "three Rs" he teaches is relocation—moving into certain neighborhoods and investing in them.

Jeremiah's words are in the same vein. Through this prophet, God tells his people, "You've relocated *physically* to Babylon, but you haven't relocated your *hearts.*" God is calling today for a movement of radical, cross-shaped urban followers who do more than relocate their jobs and families to cities—they bring their hearts as well. God wants a revolutionary movement of urban missionaries who love cities and invest in the city.

Extend your stay! I remember well the couple in our church who had been attending only about six weeks when they said, "We're only going to be here a year, but we're going to become members of a church anyway. We want to invest in this community *now*." During that one year, God prompted them to stay and invest for another year, and then another. I've also seen individuals who *don't* invest in community, even though they're in the city for some time—because they're unsure how long they'll stay. Invest! Cities need people with roots.

Jim Collins, author of the bestselling *Good to Great*, has written about the dangers of short-term thinking. He calls it the "Stockdale Paradox," named after Vice Admiral James Stockdale, a Vietnam veteran and POW. Over an eight-year period, Stockdale was tortured more than twenty times and saw many of his colleagues die through the torture and detention. But his fellow soldiers died not just of abuse but of false hope.

Stockdale told Collins, "I never lost faith in the end of the story, I never doubted not only that I would get out, but also that I would prevail in the end and turn the experience into the defining event of my life, which, in retrospect, I would not trade."

Meanwhile, those who didn't survive, Stockdale said, were "the optimists . . . the ones who said, 'We're going to be out by Christmas.' And Christmas would come, and Christmas would go. Then they'd say, 'We're going to be out by Easter.' And Easter would come, and Easter would go. And then Thanksgiving, and then it would be Christmas again. And they died of a broken heart."

Stockdale added,

> You must never confuse faith that you will prevail in the end—which you can never afford to lose—with the discipline to confront the most brutal facts of your current reality, whatever they might be.

Life is difficult. As Christians we know that the cross is a part of our lives. God's plans require embracing the difficulties and joys of our situations and walking by his timetable. The false prophets of hope could deliver only short-term dreams to the Israelites.

It raises the question: Why do we have such a short-term vision—for ourselves, and for our cities? What if we invested in very long-term plans? What if we weren't put off by the hardships?

THE PURSUIT OF *SHALOM*

Jeremiah's next words are especially potent. Here in Jeremiah 29:7, the Hebrew word *shalom*, with all its rich meaning, is found three times (translated as "welfare"):

> . . . seek the welfare of the city where I have sent you into exile, and pray to the LORD on its behalf, for in its welfare you will find your welfare.

Notice once more the hand of God here, emphasized again. In this verse he speaks of their new location not simply as "Babylon" but as "the city where I have sent you into exile." God himself was the maker and designer of their urban exile; he's reminding them again, *I myself have placed you there.* The reason for their captivity was of course God's discipline and wrath toward Israel for her past idolatry and disobedience; but simply to be reminded that their Lord, Israel's God, was in charge of everything everywhere could mean great comfort for them—as well as for us. He wants them to know that he's still *with* them.

Even more striking in this verse are the two imperatives, followed by a breathtaking promise.

God's people are given two tasks in regard to their new and unwanted location amid the very people who had oppressed them: to seek their *shalom*, and to pray for them.

Pursuing this *shalom* was like reweaving the city's social fabric. In Babylon, as in our cities today, the threads of the social fabric are easily unraveled. But God's people should seek to reweave them into patterns of wholeness and completeness. For their neighbors all around, they were to aim for the restoration of all manner of broken relationships: one's relationship with others, one's relationship with one's self, and one's relationship to the world. All these needed to be made right; that's what God's people are told to be about.

For true *shalom,* cities must be filled with families. Cities break down when families break down—when fathers leave, when teenagers have babies, when restless youths find their place in gangs. Daniel Burnham, author of the *Plan of Chicago,* "thought always of the city as a place for men and women to live and for children to grow up in; and his chief idea was to make conditions for working healthy and agreeable, and facilities for recreation both abundant and available."[9] That squares with God's idea for the city as well.

The second imperative in Jeremiah 29:7—to pray for their city— involves something that always exposes our true heart toward our location. If we truly care, if we're genuinely concerned for those around us, we'll pray for them.

Holy Trinity, our church in Chicago, is a Christ-rooted, city-focused church—and therefore we believe strongly in prayer on our city's behalf. I often take prayer walks in our city, spending a couple of hours walking the streets and talking to God about what's needed for our city. Every week, multiple groups of us meet in homes around the city for the same purpose. Because of Christ, we're *for* our city; we want what's best for Chicago—in her homes, in her schools, in her hospitals, in her workplaces. We want to see Chicago filled with families who love Christ and are absolutely, wholeheartedly devoted to him, and who will live a gospel life in their urban surroundings.

It's all part of the plan for the spiritual transformation of Chicago that we and other Chicago churches have been called to by God. The One who rules over Jerusalem and over Babylon is also the One who rules over Chicago. He's the One who brings the goodness, the completeness, the healing, the wholeness. He is Lord, and he is concerned. And so we pray and work and serve.

And we do it joyfully. We actually love this city. When the "el" goes by (that's Chicago's rapid transit system), it sounds almost like a waterfall in the mountains, and you can just let that sound roll over you, beautifully invigorating. Why? Because we love to see people moving; we love to see the welfare evidenced in people finding work and moving around. And we continue seeking that welfare as we envision and participate in the reweaving of this city's social fabric.

Reverberating down through the ages, Jeremiah's letter confirms that God's strategy is to have his people lead the way in increasing the city's *shalom*. And *shalom* is not passive, but active and organic. To seek their city's welfare would require looking out for others all around them, caring for them, serving and helping them, and pursuing their healing and security and prosperity.

In Jeremiah's words we find a beautiful and foundational strategy from God for what his people are to *do* in every place we find ourselves. Our natural tendency may be to "leave the city to itself," but Jeremiah gives us a godly vision for strategically investing ourselves wherever the Lord sends us.

A SHOCKING PROMISE

There's also a promise in Jeremiah 29:7, expressed in terms that must have shocked the people who received it. Concerning the city of Babylon the Lord promised this: "in its welfare you will find your welfare." Yes, God promises his people *shalom*, but this blessing would be wrapped up in the *shalom* of their captor—in the well-being of Babylon.

How amazing! The peace and good of God's people wasn't something autonomous and independent, disconnected from the condition of the larger city surrounding them; no, the two were inseparable—inextricably and intricately intertwined. The *shalom* of each and every individual among God's people would be bound up in the *shalom* of their city.

It's a promise that reveals God's heart behind his overall aim and purpose for people in the city. It's also a promise that, in our post-resurrection perspective, strongly calls for the gospel to be woven into all we do. Ultimate *shalom* for the citizen of any city is impossible without Christ.

We saw the centrality of preaching in the last chapter, but it's worth restating here: *repentance* is essential to peace with God, and this repentance is what preaching is designed to provoke. Moreover, the peace brought about by this preaching is profound and eternal. Paul puts it well: "Therefore, since we have been justified by faith, *we have peace with God through our Lord Jesus Christ*. Through him we have also obtained access by faith into this grace in which we stand, and we rejoice in hope of the glory of God" (Rom. 5:1–3). Here's a peace that lasts far longer than seventy years!

Our investment in our cities must be infused by the gospel. The cross and the resurrection make all the difference, because they offer genuine peace with God. In that peace, and in the Holy Spirit's power, we seek our city's welfare while we live a gospel life.

THE LONGER VIEW

What our cities need is a radical, vibrant, gospel-renewed, long-term, communal commitment to transformation on the part of faithful believers. Unfortunately, as disciples of Jesus, or simply as wandering urbanites, we often have only a short-term view, a project mind-set, and an individual mentality in regard to our cities. We'd rather consume than invest; we'd rather just visit than stay and be fruitful.

God's plans are different. God's plans always extend much farther and longer than ours.

Jeremiah's letter to the Jewish exiles goes on to state that their Babylonian captivity would last not two years, as the false prophet Hananiah had rashly predicted, but *seventy*:

> For thus says the LORD: When seventy years are completed for Babylon, I will visit you, and I will fulfill to you my promise and bring you back to this place. (Jer. 29:10)

God was giving his people a seventy-year vision and strategy for their existence in their new and hostile environment. Most of us tend to look ahead only several months or perhaps a few years. Some people, especially young adults, move to a city and think, *I'll probably be here for only a year or two*—so they don't invest. Their mind-set is to just cruise along, to not engage significantly. There's great danger in that kind of temporary mind-set, and it drains away our potential for influence.

But God helps his people see beyond the horizon. Through Jeremiah's words he shows us still today that a vision for gospel-change in our cities requires a long-term perspective and commitment—which in turn requires our radical resolve.

This type of thinking doesn't jibe with modern culture, which is increasingly short-term and instantaneous in perspective. We're a culture of fast food and ever-faster technology, but Jeremiah calls us to take a broader, longer, slower view.

ALL ABOUT HEART

It's in that immediate context that the famously reassuring promise of Jeremiah 29:11 is then spoken. Listen to it again:

> For I know the plans I have for you, declares the LORD, plans for welfare [*shalom*] and not for evil, to give you a future and a hope.

Following up this encouragement, the letter then focuses immediately on the right condition of people's hearts in responding to such a promise from God:

> Then you will call upon me and come and pray to me, and I will hear you. You will seek me and find me, when you *seek me with all your heart.* I will be found by you, declares the LORD, and I will restore your fortunes and gather you from all the nations and all the places where I have driven you, declares the LORD, and I will bring you back to the place from which I sent you into exile. (29:12–14)

This raises a critically important issue for all of us: *How is your heart?* How hard is your heart, how soft is your heart—in terms of what God is doing and saying? In the depths of your heart, how much are you genuinely willing to invest in the city, or wherever God has called you?

This was God's message in Jeremiah's time for a displaced and dejected people who had physically relocated to Babylon but had left their hearts behind. Now God was telling each one, "Relocate your *heart* there as well." Ultimately, of course, our heart is to be set on the *next* city, the eternal city, but the way we live here and now—through investment in our earthly city, in dependence on God's direction—signifies our longing for the heavenly city.

God is calling today for a movement of radical, cross-centered urban dwellers who not only find jobs and move families to cities, but who, out of loyalty to Christ, transfer their *hearts* there as well.

What is God calling *you* to do in regard to the city? Not everyone is called to the city long-term. But perhaps *you* are. Ask yourself: am I called to be one who invests in the city?

NO LITTLE PLANS

Some of the most famous words of *Plan of Chicago* author Daniel Burnham were these:

Make no little plans; they have no magic to stir men's blood and probably themselves will not be realized. Make big plans; aim high in hope and work, remembering that a noble, logical diagram once recorded will never die, but long after we are gone will be a living thing, asserting itself with ever-growing insistency. Remember that our sons and grandsons are going to do things that would stagger us. Let your watchword be order and your beacon beauty.[10]

God's plan for his exiled people in Babylon was far from little. And that's true of his plan for people in our cities of today and tomorrow as well.

If Jeremiah were on earth today to see the people of God scattered throughout every country and city of the world, it would stagger him to see the multiplication. He had written to God's people, "Do not decrease, but multiply," and by God's grace and the power of the gospel of Christ Jesus, this has indeed happened.

We all need purpose; we all need a vision. We need to know where we're going—so we need a *plan*. Therefore God inspired his prophet to write this letter, so that Jeremiah could say, "Let me give you a plan—a seventy-year plan. It's pretty simple: *Invest and build community*. Save money, buy a house, meet your neighbor, grow a family." Unlike many perspectives about urban settings today, Jeremiah's outlook is neither overly pessimistic nor overly idealistic or utopian. It's a durable model for intentional investment. It's compelling—and it's urgently needed.

For who will rebuild cities in the right way, in the way that truly channels God's gifts of *shalom,* if Christians don't? Who will be the instruments to bring God's healing touch to the social problems of the city, if Christians don't? Who will seek the *shalom* of the city if Christians don't? If God's people fail to step up, then it will only be the dealers of greed and avarice and sexual exploitation who build and define our cities.

Yet God also promises that "the earth will be filled with the knowledge of the glory of the LORD as the waters cover the sea" (Hab. 2:14). It's true for all the earth, and that means cities too. I can't wait!

So set your eyes on a farther horizon. One day the new city will come down from heaven to replace whichever one you live in now. Keep the eyes of your heart set on that new and coming city, as you meanwhile seek the welfare of the city where God has planted you. Invest in *that* city

... while seeking the next. In faithfulness to God's call, build relationships. Establish homes. Fall in love and marry, and raise children. And live single-mindedly for Christ.

A CLOSING PRAYER

Our Father,

We are amazed at your plans. That you would call your people to serve their enemies astounds us; until we remember again that you served us when we were your enemies. We thank you that Jesus lived his life not for himself, but to lose it for others, and to sacrifice for others.

When we look inside, we see the thorns and the brambles of our own hearts, how overgrown they are with selfishness and self-centeredness. It's impossible for us to think about living for shalom—except that your Son has come to bring shalom for us.

Thank you for the peace we have with you through the blood of Christ. Start with our hearts again—amaze them with your shalom—that we might bear that message to others. Father, raise up a people for the cities of our world, to invest, to share, to speak of who you are, to share Christ. In every city, encourage your people to look to the One who gave his life for them. Cause us to know the depth of his power, the power of his Spirit.

Bring peace to our neighborhoods. Bring fathers back to their sons and daughters. Restore families. We pray that you would reduce senseless violence, put an end to our abortion industry, increase adoption, mentor the unwanted, and renew families.

Spread the love of Christ in the city, for it is in his name that we pray, Amen.

PART 3

ISSUES IN CITY LIVING

Learning to Thrive in the City

*For I am not ashamed of the gospel,
for it is the power of God for salvation
to everyone who believes,
to the Jew first and also to the Greek.*

ROMANS 1:16

6

SEX AND THE CITY

Maybe mistakes are what make our fate . . .
without them what would shape our lives?
Maybe if we had never veered off course we wouldn't fall in love,
have babies, or be who we are. After all, things change,
so do cities; people come into your life and they go.

TELEVISION DIALOGUE FROM *SEX AND THE CITY*

I will rise now and go about the city,
in the streets and in the squares;
I will seek him whom my soul loves.
I sought him, but found him not.

SONG OF SOLOMON 3:2

It was 4:30, early on an August morning. In a hotel room on the edge of a Nairobi slum called Huruma, I was still sleeping when the pulsating shrieks of a woman entered my unconsciousness. I was unable at first to realize the screams were real; they were woven into a kind of twisted dream. The sound subsided, then came again with piercing reality. The woman was in pain or fear or both.

I tried to awaken, to shake off from mind and body the grog of jet lag, culture shock, and several days of slum work. I looked around; the screams had been loud enough that I literally thought they were in my room. Then the shrieks faded again.

I lay motionless for a moment, then stumbled to my fifth-floor hotel window. The bright outline of downtown Nairobi skyscrapers was miles in the distance. Directly below me, I looked across a back alley to a flat rooftop, where clotheslines flapped laundry in the wind.

There she was, lying crumpled in a heap near narrow stairs on the rooftop. She was heaving.

Then I saw him.

He stood over her, smoking a cigarette, exhaling coolly. He seemed unconcerned, looking off into the semi-darkness of Nairobi's night sky, then occasionally glancing down at her almost as if he were regarding a pile of dirty linens. Why wasn't he helping her?

Was *he* the cause of her screams?

He flicked his cigarette, nudging her with his foot.

I turned from the window and out of my room, running down five flights of stairs to the armed security guard, at his post beside a rolling steel door to the outside. I told him what I'd seen and said we needed to help.

The guard showed his teeth as he laughed. "This is Nairobi. This happens all the time in Nairobi."

To our shame, we did nothing, the guard and I.

The steel door remained firmly closed.

FUSED IMAGES

In today's human imagination, there's hardly a more powerful and prevalent combination of images than that of *sex* and *city*. The two have been fused and branded. And sometimes the connection is brutal.

But not always.

Sometimes it is literary. James Joyce joined them famously and provocatively in his massive and inventive novel *Ulysses*. Joyce overturned Victorian sensibilities not only about writing, but also about sexuality, as he wrote explicitly of Leopold Bloom's mundane misadventures, including the loss of the affections of his wife, Molly, to Blazes Boyland. Woven intricately into the everyday life of Dublin, the novel is a meandering modern odyssey of a new Odysseus searching for Penelope—only this time in the urban landscape.

More recently (and fashionably), Sarah Jessica Parker and her friends have indelibly linked desire with the urban existence in the popular *Sex and the City* TV series and films. They remind us that cities have always been a place of sexual opportunity, for better and worse. We follow young, attractive, wealthy urbanites in Manhattan and share their challenges and trials and temptations of urban romance. Take eight million people stacked on top of each other and see what happens. It's a certainty: density + passion = sexual adventurism.

It takes place in Manhattan, but it could be any city.

But love in the city isn't always merely brutal, provocative, or fashionable. Sometimes it has a simple beauty. One of the greatest joys of pastoral ministry in a city is watching things go *right* in the area of desire—seeing a young couple meet, fall in love, marry, and decide to follow Christ with their family.

SONGS FOR EVERYONE, FOR ALL TIME

The question for us in this chapter is, What does the gospel of Jesus and the Word of God have to say about living with sexual desire in the city? What does it look like to follow God in this urban generation in the area of sexuality?

There are, of course, many places we could turn in the Scriptures for answers. But one of the best places to explore is also one of the most unusual books in the entire Bible—the Song of Solomon or the Song of Songs (both titles derive from the opening verse: "The Song of Songs, which is Solomon's"). It isn't primarily an instructional or historical book (like much of the rest of Scripture), and in fact it hardly mentions God. It's rather a work of art—a rich collection of tastefully erotic love songs, to be precise. "As a work of literature of singular beauty and power, it stands on its own feet."[1]

The poetry of desire is landscaped in both rural and urban settings. The Song of Solomon speaks of the almost reckless power of awakened love that has its own mind, its own trajectories, its own plans. It displays the intoxicating power of human love and sexuality.

These songs may well have been originally written to be sung at ancient wedding celebrations, as the bride and groom prepared to enter physical intimacy on their first night together:

> The cheerful merriment of a wedding feast, with the wine flowing freely, provided a relaxed occasion in which it was not improper to celebrate the love and kisses and union of the happy couple. But this is not to suppose that the Song is bawdy or vulgar in any way. Its unembarrassed use of metaphor and allusion demonstrates the warmth

and vitality of the God-given joys of love. It was not a thing to be hidden away in a corner, as though there were something furtive or indecent about it all, but a matter that could be brought out openly in the light and a cause for public celebration.[2]

Sometimes urbanites regard God as some cosmic prude for whom expressions of human passion and sexuality would only make him uncomfortable or even ashamed. Anyone with this view should dive fully into the Song of Solomon. This God-inspired book "is a rhapsody of love: an outpouring of the words and feelings of people who are experiencing human, sexual love with all its pains and pleasures. It is a book for those who want to know, or to remember, what it is like to be in love."[3]

The value that God places here on human love and sexuality, along with the particular beauty and power of these love songs, gives the Song of Solomon an exalted place in Scripture. As a first-century Jewish teacher named Rabbi Aqiba exclaimed, "all the Writings are holy, but the Song of Songs is the Holy of Holies."[4]

With such a romantic focus, it's no surprise that these poems revolve around an intense relationship between a certain man and a certain woman. Both are quite young, and they're engaged to be married. He is presented with royal trappings, while she seems to be perhaps a peasant woman, though given the poetic genre, their precise identity and physical circumstances aren't centrally significant. What *is* given center stage here is simply their emotions and thoughts about each other. As one scholar suggests,

> We do not know, indeed we do not need to know, much about them. . . .
> In as much as their responses and feelings are those typical of all men
> and women in love, then we can identify with them. To that extent, they
> are real flesh and blood characters, with passion and ardor flowing in
> their veins. . . . The two lovers are Everyman and Everywoman.[5]

The couple's two voices alternate and intermingle in the poetry, and sometimes it isn't precisely clear who the speaker is.[6] On brief occasions, the voices of others—acquaintances of the lovers—come in as well, somewhat like the chorus in an ancient Greek play. But it's the young woman who speaks most often, and her passions and feelings are by far the most prominent.

The imagery employed in the songs is rich with metaphors from nature. Arising from a Near Eastern culture three thousand years ago, it can at times seem strange and even jarring to readers today with the images of mountains, spices, and apple trees. But rightly understanding this as poetry, and reading the metaphors with alert understanding, we can easily catch the intense and exalted passion these lovers possess for each other.

Their relationship unifies this work of art; it literally is a song of songs, compiled together—thus, the songs aren't necessarily sequential and may seem fragmentary.[7] Line follows line and poem follows poem in a stream-of-consciousness flow. The feelings expressed by the lovers seem to soar and dive in a rather wild and unpredictable flight—exactly the way lovers' thoughts typically do.

INTENSITY AND POWER

All of the Song of Solomon can give us poetic insight into the theme of sex and city, but let's dip in at just a few places to get a stronger feel.

After the opening title-verse, the woman's voice begins the first song:

Let him kiss me with the kisses of his mouth!
For your love is better than wine. (Song 1:2)

The wine imagery is appropriate; there's definitely a headiness to the drinking of erotic love and romance. That's something countless couples have known. Later in the book, the power of awakened romantic love will be compared also to a raging fire:

Many waters cannot quench love,
neither can floods drown it. (8:7)

As the song at the beginning continues to unfold, an interplay of the man and woman's attraction to each other effectively draws us in. "In listening to the Song, we find that it is speaking not only *to* us but *about* us. We are captivated and drawn into its movement and ambience. Our imaginations are stimulated and we begin to identify with the lovers on their journey of love, of self-discovery and of fulfillment."[8]

We soon see the feelings of the young man and young woman intensify, along with hints of tension in the situation. We hear the woman affirm how the young man has "brought me to the banqueting house, and his banner over me was love" (2:4); a few lines later she quickly adds, "I am sick with love" (2:5).

She excitedly acknowledges the man's intimate presence: "His left hand is under my head, and his right hand embraces me!" (2:6). But then she steps outside this scene to give instruction to others:

> I adjure you, O daughters of Jerusalem,
>> by the gazelles or the does of the field,
> that you not stir up or awaken love
>> until it pleases. (2:7)

Looking to nature, her oath by the "gazelles" and "does of the field" constitutes a kind of warning. These "daughters of Jerusalem" she addresses seem to particularly represent all the young single women of her community, and especially her close friends. But in a song that so happily and even playfully celebrates romance, her counsel to these friends is quite serious and invites careful reflection: *love is not to be aroused until the proper time.*[9]

By virtue of repetition, this advice emerges as a key theme in the Song of Solomon, declared three times (we'll see it again in 3:5 and 8:4). There's something about the intoxicating power of romantic love that calls for wisdom and discretion. To a culture that refers to sexual intimacy as "hooking up," this advice may seem foreign. In ministering to men and women I've seen this power firsthand many times—in positive and negative ways, with men and women who have found their love overtaken by passion. The young woman's advice in the Song of Solomon is worth hearing again.

EXPOSED IN A DREAM

Having gotten a taste of the Song as a whole, let's dig deeper into two particular linked poems to explore love and desire from a biblical perspective—in a way that I hope will be helpful for the urban generation.

Both poems (in Song 3:1–5 and 5:2–8) happen to have the city for a backdrop. But they're included in the Song of Songs not to teach us about cities or even love in cities, but to teach us about the power of erotic love.

The first poem might be titled "Love Lost and Found." It unfolds with what appears to be a dream segment. The woman says,

On my bed by night
I sought him whom my soul loves;
    I sought him, but found him not. (3:1)

We picture her, asleep or awake, turning to find her lover. In our dreams, our deepest insecurities and fears often take control. That could be what's happening here; the young woman is fully and deeply attracted to the young man, but she doesn't yet sense that the relationship is fixed and lasting. So in her dream she finds herself frustrated in a search for him.

She even does something that in her culture would be improper and unrealistic—she goes out alone in the night to find him:

I will rise now and go about the city,
    in the streets and in the squares;
I will seek him whom my soul loves.
    I sought him, but found him not. (3:2)

Here we see again the urban setting. In city streets and squares, she fails to find this young man she loves, but she does encounter other people, and enlists their help:

The watchmen found me
    as they went about in the city.
"Have you seen him whom my soul loves?" (3:3)

Later, we'll meet these urban watchmen again in rough circumstances. Meanwhile, the woman's dream makes its way to a happy resolution—all the way to envisioning the physical consummation of their relationship:

Scarcely had I passed them
    when I found him whom my soul loves.
I held him, and would not let him go
    until I had brought him into my mother's house,
    and into the chamber of her who conceived me. (3:4)

And yet, reaching this happy fulfillment, once again she injects into the song her solemn advice for others:

> I adjure you, O daughters of Jerusalem,
>> by the gazelles or the does of the field,
> that you not stir up or awaken love
>> until it pleases. (3:5)

MORE TENSION

The second dream-like sequence follows a grand wedding celebration. This poem echoes and deepens the tensions we observed earlier in the woman's restless dream of seeking her lost lover.

As the song opens in Song 5:2, it seems likely that she's dreaming. Perhaps this dream occurred before their wedding and is now being recalled, or maybe it happened after the wedding, reflecting her continuing inner restlessness. We don't know, and it doesn't matter much; the scene plays out consistently with "the whole tenor of the poem, which is to portray feelings and emotions against a bare minimum of supportive narrative framework."[10]

This new song begins:

> I slept, but my heart was awake.
> A sound! My beloved is knocking. (5:2)

Alone in bed, she sleeps, yet she's awake; it's intriguingly vague. There's a sound, either imagined or real, of someone rapping on the door. She recognizes who this is because he quickly calls out from the other side:

> Open to me, my sister, my love,
>> my dove, my perfect one,
> for my head is wet with dew,
>> my locks with the drops of the night. (5:2)

"Open to me," he says, his words full of poetic ambiguity. The evening dew on the young man's head symbolizes sensuous anticipation and desire.

Heightening the erotic drama, the woman is unclothed, having freshly bathed:

> I had put off my garment;
>> how could I put it on?
> I had bathed my feet;
>> how could I soil them? (5:3)

She appears innocently unprepared for her lover's advance. Why does she hesitate? Is she playing a coy lover's game? Is she asserting independence? Is she seductively trying to heighten desire by making him wait?

The hesitation evaporates with the further sound of his seeking entry.

> My beloved put his hand to the latch,
>> and my heart was thrilled within me. (5:4)

Full of double entendre, the intoxication begins again. The fire is being rekindled. Anticipation stirs. Her perspective changes, and now she acts:

> I arose to open to my beloved,
>> and my hands dripped with myrrh,
> my fingers with liquid myrrh,
>> on the handles of the bolt. (5:5)

Her hands poetically drip with sweet-smelling spice, perhaps to anoint him after letting him in; but more likely the image is intended to add to the erotic mood. She's fully awake now, fully responsive. If this were a movie scene, the background music would be swelling.

But her arrival at the door brings an unwelcome discovery:

> I opened to my beloved,
>> but my beloved had turned and gone.
> My soul failed me when he spoke.
> I sought him, but found him not;
>> I called him, but he gave no answer. (5:6)

The passage describes well the disappointment of a missed encounter and the tenuousness of love. There's deep dismay at the cost of her delay; her "soul failed." This is love unfulfilled. She hesitated, and now he's gone. In the earlier poem in chapter 3, he was lost but then found—here he is lost and not found. Her agony lengthens as she turns in every direction to look for him and calls out his name to the empty darkness.

This is the elusiveness of romantic love—an awakening of desire, the ecstasy of anticipation, then occasionally (or even often) an overwhelming sense of loss. Doesn't this fit with many of our urban fears, both rational and irrational? *What if I wait too long?* Love is like some train to catch at the right moment. Miss the train, and it departs without you.

As the poem continues, she is filled with foreboding. He *was* at the door, before he was gone. Or was he ever really there? And will he ever return?

BRUTALITY

What happens next to the woman is abrupt and startling; cast in the urban landscape, it evokes a foreboding and ominous mood. The "watchmen" who were in her dream before make a repeat appearance, but this time the scene lurches into terror:

> The watchmen found me
> as they went about in the city;
> they beat me, they bruised me,
> they took away my veil,
> those watchmen of the walls. (5:7)

This woman seeks her love in the city, and instead finds brutality.

It seems to come out of nowhere. What had started as an idyllic dream turns suddenly into a horrifying nightmare. One imagines the guards laughing: "This is Jerusalem; what do you expect?" Instead of resting in her lover's comfort, she's caught up in chaos. Here in this tender book, longing for intimacy is interrupted by the harsh realities of lust and violence within a city.

The imagery of the "veil" suggests purity. Since she speaks of her "veil" being taken away, the poem may hint these men sexually assaulted her. At the very least she was beaten and bruised, her clothing torn, her spirit shattered.

The poem, whether set as a nightmare or a wild fantasy, carries a warning to us all: *Be aware!* Awakened love has an elusive, almost reckless power. This is not a meditation on the dangers of the city, but on the complexity of love.

This kind of brutality in erotic love is *not* God's desire, either in the urban context or elsewhere. Yet the Bible is realistic; while it holds out the beautiful power of romance, it also shows the crazy, sometimes disturbing sway of erotic love.

All of us know women and men for whom a similar nightmare has unfolded. We hear often of the abuse of power in the arena of sexuality. One of the most disturbing aspects of counseling within a church is the stories of women who haven't yet fully healed from being taken advantage of by some trusted teacher or family friend. Another of the most horrifying realities of modern sexuality is how pornography and lust keep so many in bondage.

There's an intriguing image toward the end of the Song of Solomon that seems almost too quaint in our modern, sexualized urban culture to be true. We hear words from protective brothers (or possibly from the covenant community):

> What shall we do for our sister
>   on the day when she is spoken for?
> If she is a wall,
>   we will build on her a battlement of silver,
> but if she is a door,
>   we will enclose her with boards of cedar. (Song 8:8–9)

Those speaking here, like older brothers wanting to shield their sister's purity, are a stark contrast to "those watchmen of the walls"; rather than exploit, they guard.

Awakened love can be absolutely brutal. Even without the violence, there's very often heartbreak and pain. These particular poems in Song of Songs tell us that aroused love can go off the rails, hurtling in a dangerous trajectory no one can stop. That's love and longing in the city.

Love has a power that can sap and wilt one's will. The dream sequence closes with this request:

> I adjure you, O daughters of Jerusalem,
>   if you find my beloved,
> that you tell him
>   I am sick with love. (5:8)

Romantic love's power is so varied, the woman speaks of it here as something draining her strength.

MORE DELIGHT, FURTHER WARNING

What is the message of these poems? It's one we need to hear, as it is repeated again toward the end of the Song, to echo in our minds:

> I adjure you, O daughters of Jerusalem,
>   that you not stir up or awaken love
>   until it pleases. (Song 8:4)

Throughout the Song we read of desire—and power. The woman later affirms that "love is strong as death," that it has "flashes of fire, the very flame of the Lord" (8:6). Proverbs 6:27 asks, "Can a man carry fire next to his chest and his clothes not be burned?"

The woman says also that love is wholly priceless, so that "if a man offered for love all the wealth of his house, he would be utterly despised" (Song 8:7). By comparison, we're told about a vineyard, owned by King Solomon, worth thousands of pieces of silver; yet its value is as nothing compared to the woman's own "vineyard"—and by this point we know well what she's referring to. Romantic love, physically enjoyed, sustains a supreme value—even though caution is required.

But we can't escape also this poem's message that the power of erotic love, once awakened, needs the protective power of the chaste and faithful covenant community—because love and passion can have a brutal underbelly.

Wendell Berry, the agrarian poet, novelist, and essayist, expresses it in these words:

Because of our determination to separate sex from the practice of love in marriage and in family and community life, our public sexual morality is confused, sentimental, bitter, complexly destructive and hypocritical."[11]

THE ALTERNATIVE POWER OF COVENANT COMMUNITY

While the sheer density of cities makes them cultural magnets for romance, love, and sensuality, their added anonymity often shapes them to be places for hurt and loss as well. Countless city-dwellers have experienced an awakened love that ends in frustration, pain, isolation, and sometimes even violence and brutality.

I've seen this power many times. I'll never forget the phone call I received about six years ago from Ed, a young man new to the city, when he had hit rock bottom. Though he's now happily married and has seen God bless him with a beautiful wife and a young son, in high school he had been introduced to pornography. He thought he could manage its allure, but in college the power of lust fully captured him and broke his control. Viewings on his computer became a daily habit. They grew more intense as the years went on.

When he began dating the young woman who is now his wife, he wanted to break free from the power of his addiction. He couldn't bear the thought of bringing this habit into his marriage. That's when he asked me for help.

I promised him that the gospel—in the context of covenant community—could set him free.

Through a process of confession, accountability, and monitoring—all in the gospel of grace—not only is Ed now free from this power, but he wakes up early on Saturday mornings to lead other men into freedom from sexual idolatry. That doesn't mean he's never tempted or never stumbles. But he's released from its power.

What made the difference for him, and for others like him whom he has helped? The answer is the gospel—God's power to free us, through the gracious application of the Spirit, not just from the penalty of sin, but from being ruled by sin's power.

That difference was also due to the gospel being lived out in the context of covenant community. Ed made sure he told others around him, including his community group leader, that he needed help. Now he "adjures" his brothers, with the gospel at the center, not to awaken what they know they can't control.

This is a pattern we've seen repeated over the years: men and women caught by a power that intoxicates like wine—then set free to lead and serve God with joy.

The Song of Songs celebrates the sweetness of love but also realistically portrays its power.

It is our gospel-hope that God, in every city, is raising up "sons and daughters of Jerusalem" like Ed, like the men he leads on Saturday mornings, and like the men and women in his community group. What our cities need most, in the area of sexuality, is for the gospel's strength to be more powerful than even our passionate desires.

When a gospel-giving, covenant-extending God surrounds broken people with redemptive community, healing occurs. God's Word repairs the broken. Cities, with their sexual allure and brutality, profoundly need redemptive covenant communities to strengthen men and women in developing enduring, beautiful, and faithful relationships.

For our cities to awaken spiritually, we need to take seriously the power of love—for good and harm—which is sometimes overlooked or ignored. We've all heard Paul McCartney tell us throughout the years, "Love is all you need." The Song of Songs, seen in the scope of Scripture as a whole, says love *isn't* all we need—unless that love is God's. The Song yearns for this deeper love that comes with covenant commitments. In the Hebrew Scriptures, this covenant love is called *hesed*. It is God's covenant love, a durable, persevering, protecting, joyful love based on a promise "never to leave or forsake" (see Heb. 13:5).

It is, in a sense, what the woman in the Song asks for when she says,

Set me as a seal upon your heart,
    as a seal upon your arm. (Song 8:6)

This seal is public—a covenant made before the community. It's celebrated in chapter 3 in a scene with the royal carriage guarded by sixty sword-bearing warriors, when Solomon is portrayed as being crowned "on the day of his wedding, on the day of the gladness of his heart" (3:11). Romantic and erotic love needs the *hesed* commitment of "till death do us part." Without this, erotic urban love leaves disappointment, loss, and woundedness. The Song of Solomon tells us that erotic love within the bounds of *one man* and *one woman*—for *life*—is intoxicatingly powerful. In pop-culture language, the request to "set me as a seal" (8:6) is saying, *Put a ring on it!* Love needs the sealing context of *covenant*.

THE GREATER LOVE

While we reject an exclusively allegorical interpretation of the Song of Songs, this book does leave us longing for a greater, more complete love. It hints of the deepest longings for love that each of us has for relational intimacy that endures.

In *The Mystery of Marriage*, Mike Mason counsels us not to underestimate the importance, the cost, and the impact of lifelong commitment:

> We are not simply moving in with someone we think it might be fun to live with. Rather, we are giving our prior assent to a whole chain reaction of trials, decisions, transformations, and personal cataclysms which, once they are done with us, may leave us not only changed almost beyond recognition, but marked nearly as deeply as by a religious conversion. And this is just as it ought to be.

Love requires this commitment because of its power to *change* us:

> Love being the most potent of forces, it is hardly surprising that the most overwhelming experiences of life should be those of being in love—first with God and then with another human being.
>
> There is no trick of a magician or spell of a witch doctor, no drug or mesmerism or bribery or torture or coercion that can compare in power with the force for change unleashed in the human breast through the touch of love. . . . When Love knocks at the door, what sort of man does not drop whatever he is doing at once and come running?[12]

Ultimately the Bible pictures God's love as a *pursuing* love, a pursuit famously described by C. S. Lewis. His conversion, he recalls, was as someone "brought in kicking, struggling, resentful, and darting in every direction for a chance of escape." He sets the scene:

You must picture me alone in that room . . . night after night, feeling, whenever my mind lifted even for a second from my work, the steady, unrelenting approach of Him whom I so earnestly desired not to meet. That which I greatly feared had at last come upon me. . . . I gave in, and admitted that God was God, and knelt and prayed: perhaps, that night, the most dejected and reluctant convert in all England.[13]

This is what's remarkable about gospel Christianity. God comes to us. God invades. God awakens us to his love.

The gospel gives us a picture of love that moves beyond loss and brutality. In the New Testament, God in Christ is pictured as a husband—a sacrificial man of covenant, *hesed* love. The reality of the gospel is that One is brutalized for the protection of another. The gospel pictures us together—God's people, the church—as a woman, brutalized by the horrors of sin, crumpled, broken, sought beyond the edge of safety, found and loved again for the sake of the gospel. It's the love we see in this familiar passage on marriage:

. . . Christ loved the church and gave himself up for her, that he might sanctify her, having cleansed her by the washing of water with the word, so that he might present the church to himself in splendor, without spot or wrinkle or any such thing, that she might be holy and without blemish. (Eph. 5:25–27)

The severity of Christ's giving up himself for us—enduring the horrifying wrath of God—makes any brutality in the Song of Songs or in Nairobi seem but a flash of horror.

Today, it's in the area of sexuality where we especially need the gospel to penetrate our lives and our cities. This is not about mere morality, but about *redemption*. Our cities and our citizens need the redeeming, forgiving, empowering love of Christ.

Thomas Jefferson once declared (from his quiet estate in the country), "I view great cities as a pestilence to the morals, the health and the liberties of man." But our cities themselves are not the pestilence. The pestilence is within—in the hearts of brutalizing watchmen, of complacent guards and pastors, and even of crumpled victims. Cities are just concentrations of people who carry a pestilence inside them. It's not the city that's corrupt; it's all our hearts that are corrupt. Our own stained souls are what leads to brutality in the city.

Hebrews 13:12 tells us how "Jesus . . . suffered outside the gate in order to sanctify the people through his own blood." In his suffering outside Jerusalem's gates, Jesus knew unspeakable brutality and violence, even to the extent of encompassing the worst of all the evil inflicted in all the world's history. And he did it, this verse says, "to sanctify the people"—making them pure, making them holy, ready for presentation to himself.

The gospel takes seriously the power of love, lust, longing, and loss. It recasts humanity's story as one of a people lost to the wrong loves, and of a God willing to overcome *all* to find us. Jesus, the Son of God and Savior of sinners, left his throne in heaven and *sought* us, then died a violent death outside the city—and that death purifies all who will now look to him in faith. It's an exchange—each of us can give over all our violence and corruption and receive from Jesus *his* purity.

Our cities, our neighbors, and our hearts need to be awakened with this love of God in Christ. As Lewis has famously suggested, the problem with our loves is not that they're too strong, but that they're too weak.[14] We need this *hesed*, covenant love of God. Such self-giving love is the only cleansing powerful enough to bring true and lasting healing from the brutality of erotic love gone awry—both for those who have inflicted it and for those who are victims. Christ *knows* our affliction, our wandering, our bitterness. We do *not* have to be consumed by it—because *he* was.

Christ has heard our voice, has arisen, and has opened the door. Christ has gone willingly into the streets. He was beaten, disrobed, disfigured—and finally, outside the city, he was put to death and buried. But he rose again! And he declares a new way of living. Not of being controlled by erotic passion, but of being controlled by the power of the Spirit, and being cleansed by his blood.

The gospel gives us the love we have been longing for.

A CLOSING PRAYER

Our Father in heaven,

We thank you that in your creativity and generosity, you have given us the gift of human love in its expression—the love of a mother, of a father, of a family, and the brotherly love of a covenant community around us. We thank you also, Lord, for giving to us marital love as well—of a husband and wife—and for the intimacy, wonder, and power of sexuality.

We admit to you that we, with our culture, can idolize sensuality. We objectify others, seek our own pleasure, and do not always honor you as we ought.

Thank you for redeeming us from the patterns and ways of this world. Protect the men and women around us from the sometimes brutalizing power of sexuality without restraint.

We thank you for your Son, for his respect and honor for women, for his calling us into a family with you.

In the name of Christ we pray,

Amen.

7

ETHNICITY AND THE CITY

We continue to live in a society where race matters.

JACOB L. VIGDOR

There is neither Jew nor Greek,
there is neither slave nor free,
there is no male and female,
for you are all one in Christ Jesus.

GALATIANS 3:28

Paul had always wanted to preach in Rome. It wasn't until the end of his life that he got there, and then as a prisoner—though that didn't stop him from preaching (Acts 28:16, 30–31). Before he came to that city, he wrote the most magisterial theological book ever written. No other book, and very likely no Scripture, has been more widely used by God than the book of Romans. Half a millennium ago, an essentially new civilization in Europe was given birth through a movement that centered on these words:

> For I am not ashamed of the gospel, for it is the power of God for salvation to everyone who believes, to the Jew first and also to the Greek. For in it the righteousness of God is revealed from faith for faith, as it is written, "The righteous shall live by faith." (Rom. 1:16–17)

For Martin Luther and his followers, as well as the other pioneers of the Reformation, this powerful text from the apostle Paul reinvigorated Christianity with the freshly understood concept of our being justified by faith alone, through grace alone, solely through our Lord and Savior Jesus Christ, who was offered up for our sins.

It's a crucial passage on the doctrine of salvation, on the opening page of a letter to people living in what was then the greatest city in all of world history. But seen in context, it is also a text which, surprisingly, can help us to follow God more faithfully in our complex and dizzyingly diverse urban generation, particularly in the area of ethnicity.

Here's a question to consider: how might viewing ethnicity *from the perspective of the gospel* help bring Christ more faithfully to the center of our cities? Romans has more to say on that than we might think.

A FAITH FOR ALL

Paul's famous words in Romans 1:16 deliver a succinct knockout blow to human sufficiency in salvation. But the context is intriguing. Paul places his claim—about salvation by faith alone through Christ alone—squarely among comments related to ethnicity. Romans 1:14–16 provides an original yet revolutionary way to think of race in our urban generation.

Honestly, this seems strange. Romans is a *theological* treatise, is it not? Why would Paul introduce ethnicity or class *here*; and what can we learn from it?

Notice especially three statements on ethnicity here:

- Paul says that the gospel "is the power of God for salvation to *everyone* who believes, *to the Jew first and also to the Greek.*" (Rom. 1:16). Priority is given to the Jews since, historically, God called Abraham first; Jesus went first to Jews; Paul went first to the synagogues.
- A second reference to ethnicity or class comes as Paul tells why he wants to come to Rome: "I am under obligation both to Greeks and to barbarians, both to the wise and to the foolish. So I am eager to preach the gospel to you also who are in Rome" (1:14–15). Paul is *obligated* by a universal message, this gospel that he says he's "not ashamed of" (1:16).
- Another reference to ethnicity is given earlier, at the chapter's beginning, and is the source of the others. Paul claims that through Jesus he has "received grace and apostleship to bring about the obedience of faith for the sake of his name *among all the nations,*" literally *ethnesin,* "ethnic groupings" (1:5).

Why are these statements here? Why, in this great letter, this monumental theological treatise, does Paul deal with ethnicity or cultural groupings, and why is this a reason for his wanting to preach in Rome?

Paul is saying that the gospel applies to *all*. He's stating its universal relevance, declaring that the gospel alone is the way of salvation for all people. But he seems to be saying slightly more than this as well.

As developed throughout this letter, Paul carries the logic one step further: because the gospel is universally relevant (1:16–17), because salvation by grace alone through faith alone applies equally to everyone (chapters 1–8), because we're all under sin (1:18–3:31), and because Christ is Lord over every people group as well as Lord over the polar extremes of humanity (1:5; 4:17–18; 16:26)—there's a mandatory urgency that no group be neglected, that every group be represented when applying the gospel.

Rome is a particularly good place to demonstrate this. Paul urgently wants to clearly and visibly apply the gospel to the polar extremes of society—and all in between.

WHEN IN ROME

The unique opportunity for displaying this in Rome was heightened by the city's density and diversity, as reflected in Paul's stated obligation "both to Greeks and to barbarians, both to the wise and to the foolish" (Rom. 1:14).

We see here that Paul has a dual obligation to Gentiles, among whom God has called him to two main classes. The "Greeks" represented especially the cultural elite, the social and intellectual "haves" of that day; they looked down on others as "barbarians"—low-grade outsiders and have-nots. Paul adds that he was obligated "both to the wise and to the foolish" (1:14), a poetic restatement of "Greeks and barbarians" intended to make Roman prejudices more obvious. Many in the Roman empire considered Greeks to be wise and barbarians foolish.

The pervasive presence of both these classes in densely populated Rome enticed Paul's coming. In 1:13 he's saying, "So what if they're not educated? Or so what if they're even far more educated than I am? I have to preach to them all! *I have to tell them!* I want to come to Rome, the empire's capital, for God to bring a harvest there as he has among the rest of the Gentiles."

The nature of the gospel, because of the lordship of Christ, is that it *must* span differences (Rom. 14:7–11; Eph. 4:1–6). A God of Jews only, or of Greeks only, or of barbarians only, is not *Lord*. Greeks and barbarians had many gods—no one single God like Yahweh ruled them all. In Rome's cosmopolitan microcosm of the city and church, Paul saw a unique opportunity to demonstrate the culture-bridging gospel of Jesus. By carefully applying the gospel, Paul could bring the Roman church a sense of deep unity in Christ even in the midst of great diversity. Rome's need was for salvation, but also for this unity that was possible only in Christ.

Paul's declaration that he was unashamed of the gospel's power for *all* gains significance when we consider that Jews and Greeks represented Rome's two most educated classes, who through their learnedness might be ashamed of the gospel. Even on their behalf, Paul is confident in the gospel. Jews are given priority—"to the Jew first," he says here—because of historic precedence reflected in Paul's tendency to begin his ministry in any city in the synagogue. And though his mention of Greeks here might suggest *all* Gentiles, Paul appears to use the term *Greek* here because it is they, the cultural elites of that day, who tended to be ashamed at the gospel's foolish message (see 1 Cor. 1:23). Paul confirms that he bears an unashamed obligation to declare this gospel of Jesus to every kind of people.

TOWARD HARMONY

Rome was the right audience for this passion.

Paul was writing to believers in a great ancient city whose population density was comparable to that of our most crowded cities today. In the ancient world, it was unmatched for its diversity. In Rome, there were more Greeks than in any other locale on earth, and more barbarians too. Rome had all types; everyone was represented. So the believers there could not avoid the agitations caused by distinctions of race, class, and culture. For their sake, Paul courageously took a stand, emboldened by his belief in the gospel's power, relevance, and urgency. He urges them to unity.

At the end of the letter, Paul repeatedly brings in the idea of unity despite diversity. All of chapter 14 and much of chapters 12 and 15 deal with this topic. In chapter 12 he challenges "everyone among you not to think of himself more highly than he ought to think" (Rom. 12:3), and reminds them that "we, though many, are one body in Christ" (12:5). He urges Rome's believers to "live in such harmony with one another, in accord with Christ Jesus, that together you may with one voice glorify the God and Father of our Lord Jesus Christ" (Rom. 15:5–6; this call to one voice is particularly remarkable since Paul earlier declared how the testimony of God's law, to "both Jews and Greeks," is such "that every mouth may be stopped"; 3:9, 19). Paul also exhorted them to "welcome one another as Christ has welcomed you, for the glory of God" (15:5–7). Because of the gospel of grace, unity comes amid diversity.

Paul wanted to preach in Rome, but until he could do so, he would preach to them through a letter showing Jews, Greeks, and barbarians their amazing unity and equality within the church, despite their human and cultural differences. Paul saw clearly how these differences are overcome by the gospel's power. The logical outcome of the good news—even for the racial chaos of a city—is unity and harmony. For urban people clustered together like the Romans were, the gospel had—and *has*—an incomparable significance.

Paul doesn't ignore the Romans' diversity as if it didn't exist, or try to obliterate it as if to create some deracinated church, or mute their different voices so as to leave only one note sounding; rather, their differences are recognized, transcended, and *combined* to create a swelling orchestra of beauty. Because of the Spirit-empowered gospel of Jesus, they make one new harmonic song of praise for God and welcome toward all, as they joyfully serve one another. The gospel enables this by removing our hostility and giving us peace with God.

The implication for following God in our complex and diverse cities is that race, class, and ethnicity can come together in the beauty of harmony. Harmony exists only where diversity exists. Paul isn't saying that the gospel merely *transcends* ethnicity or *applies* to all cultures; he shows how the gospel solves our problem of race by dealing with the deep problems of the heart and sin; it judges, corrects, silences, and finally unifies all differences.

So if we attempt to take race *out* of the picture, we actually dim the beauty of the gospel.

Today, we often read Paul's letter to Rome as only a theological treatise, and when we come to phrases that show a particular sensitivity to social and cultural divisions, we skip over this nuance of his message—ignoring a powerful reality that our world, particularly in urban environments, is hungry for.

A TENSION POINT

Racial tension was palpable in Rome in New Testament times. In Acts 18:2, Luke mentions somewhat incidentally that Emperor Claudius "had commanded all the Jews to leave Rome," an expulsion also mentioned by the Roman historian Suetonius.[1] Imagine the effect this would have on a local church, with all its Jewish founding members banished from the city. Overnight the church would become Gentile-only, and all direct influence of Jewish culture would be eliminated.

The edict lasted for perhaps as many as five years.

Imagine also the practical questions for the Roman church after the edict was lifted and people of Jewish heritage returned. The culture clash would be inevitable and significant. Ethnic tension probably intensified.

For Roman Christians the burning question would be, How should we as Jews and Gentiles, Greeks and barbarians—in this great cosmopolitan city—get along? How do we work together for the gospel? How do we live in harmony, welcome each other, and live together despite all our cultural differences? How can we work and serve the Lord together?

This was the situation in Rome as Paul wrote his letter to them. The implications of these questions are addressed through his brilliant treatise on our universal sinfulness, the gospel's power to save all, and our oneness in Christ. Paul wasn't saying that God is color-blind, or that he himself was color-blind. He was saying that the gospel recognizes cultural differences and then transcends them with the gospel. That's why Romans can help us in the areas of race and grace, of ethnicity and complexity.

COMPLEXITY OF ETHNICITY

I'm not saying that overcoming racial or cultural differences and hostility is easy. But I am saying—and I believe Paul is as well—that when we put aside our natural tendency toward judgmentalism and superiority, and when we do it because we have a deep sense of God's amazing plan in the gospel—the result is beautiful.

In my city of Chicago, as well as in many other cities today, racial and cultural wounds run deep, still awaiting complete healing even after decades of on-the-surface progress. I've sometimes heard urbanites, especially if they're white, argue that there are no such wounds. But among my African-American friends I find that the hurt is often still profoundly felt. The wearying battles of the civil rights movement have not cured everything.

For a number of years I served on the local school council at my children's neighborhood school. A friend of mine, a woman known for speaking her mind, looked me in the eye and said, "Do you know what it feels like to be referred to as three-fifths human?" It stopped me in my tracks. No, I didn't. She was referring, of course, to our U.S. Constitution, which originally counted only three-fifths of America's slave population when determining representation of each state in Congress. That was changed, of course, with passage of the Fourteenth Amendment after the Civil War, a century and a half ago. But the pain in her voice and in her eyes was real.

In Chicago, racial woundedness goes back a long way. In 1966, when Martin Luther King Jr. chose Chicago as the place to begin his civil rights work in the north, he was shocked by the intensity of opposition to racial integration. At one particular march, protestors cried out at King, "Kill him, kill him." One threw a rock at King and knocked him to the ground. Another threw a knife. King remarked, "I have been in many demonstrations all across the south, but I can say that I have never seen—even in Mississippi and Alabama—mobs as hostile and hate filled as I've seen in Chicago." He added, "I think the people from Mississippi ought to come to Chicago to learn how to hate."[2]

AN OVERRIDING REALITY

This is the very hostility that the gospel can remove. What changed Paul? What caused him to be able to see through cultural hostility and differences to unity? The gospel so radically awakened and changed Paul that he saw through racial hostility to something else.

121

Paul was a Jewish man from a very strict Jewish background, someone who had been taught all his life to avoid dealings with Gentiles. Prior to his conversion, he would have been terribly uncomfortable associating in any way with any Gentile. According to his scruples, such actions would have made him ritually unclean.

In Paul's environment, Jews spoke of Gentiles as "dogs"—and Gentiles returned the favor. An "us versus them" mentality was entrenched.

But an overriding reality—the gospel—invaded Paul's life and changed his entire outlook.

Paul became a servant. His life was not his own. In the very first verse of his epistle to the Romans, Paul identified himself as "a servant of Christ Jesus, called to be an apostle, set apart for the gospel of God." As Christ's servant, he allowed Christ to rearrange all the priorities of his life. His new identity had been reshaped by Jesus' identity as his Lord. Paul speaks of him as "Jesus Christ our Lord" (Rom. 1:4) to emphasize that Jesus rules over all.

As an apostle of Jesus Christ, Paul understood that his particular responsibility was "to bring about the obedience of faith for the sake of his name among *all the nations*" (1:5). That is, if Christ is Lord *at* all, then he is Lord *of* all, of every people. This is why Paul asserted his "obligation" (1:14) to *everyone*; he was bound and determined to communicate the gospel to *all*.

Paul isn't saying that cultural distinctions don't matter (which they don't, of course, in coming to Christ). He is saying that penetrating cultural distinctions with the gospel *does* matter because it shows that Christ is Lord of all. Paul's ambition and calling was to offer salvation to the world and to show how wide is this rule of Christ.

Paul had this awesome responsibility, this clear duty—but it wasn't some heavy and unwelcome burden for him. No, he confessed, "I am *eager* to preach the gospel to you" (1:15). He was motivated, passionate, zealous, and inwardly compelled to preach the gospel in this superdense, super-diverse city of Rome. Paul was *excited*—because he knew the salvation and unity it could bring.

When Paul said, "I am under obligation" (1:14), this Greek term includes the concept of indebtedness. Paul viewed himself as a debtor to Christ for something that was covered and paid on his behalf. That debt was the one personally paid for him on the cross; Paul's Savior had been crucified, bearing the penalty for Paul's own sins, which included complicity in the murder of Christians. This debt bought his loyalty as Christ's slave and apostle. But Paul was also a debtor in the sense of being obligated to pass along what had been entrusted to him for the sake of others. Paul was bound, as we are, to deliver the wonderful news of Christ.

This perspective of amazing grace and mercy—coupled with joyful duty—is the background for Paul's description of himself as "a servant [or "bondservant"] of Christ Jesus" (1:1). For all the rest of his life, Paul would feel this bond of servitude and gratitude—not in any demeaning way but in a highly exalting and liberating way, because he belonged forever to One who was the Savior of the world and of his very own soul. Paul had this sense of awesome commitment to the One who paid such a price for him at the cross.

Moreover, with the same grace and mercy, Paul's Savior had now commissioned him to be his apostle—a "sent one," a messenger going out on behalf of another. Paul was telling these Roman urbanites, "I've been sent to you by the Savior of the world, by the risen King . . . by the Lord himself!"

WHO—OR WHAT—IS LORD?

The gospel helps solve the problem of race by showing clearly that Jesus is Lord of every ethnicity. This centering of Christ over all races helps us follow God faithfully in our cities when we confront racial hostility. Paul speaks emphatically here in Romans 1 of "Jesus Christ our *Lord*" and "the *Lord* Jesus Christ" (Rom. 1:4, 7). There's only one Lord, one King—and it's Jesus. *He* is sovereign and supreme over every individual as well as every people group. He's Lord over every class and culture, every race and religion, every tribe and tongue, every nationality and ethnic category, and over any alignment and assortment or distinction or division or demographic labeling whatsoever.

In the urban context, we could say that Christ is Lord over Goths and hipsters as well as businesspeople and the homeless. And because Christ is Lord over all, therefore his *gospel* is unequivocally for all—for each individual and every collection or gathering of individuals in any and all situations, anywhere and everywhere.

This is unmistakably emphasized in Scripture.

Jesus said, "This gospel of the kingdom will be proclaimed *throughout the whole world* as a testimony to *all nations*, and then the end will come" (Matt. 24:14). Before history ends, the gospel will continue to be preached, and it will someday bear fruit among *every single people group*—something that's happening in dramatic ways all around the globe, and moving toward biblical fulfillment. Believers everywhere are obeying the command of Jesus when he said, "Go into *all the world* and proclaim the gospel to *the whole creation*" (Mark 16:15). And they're remembering his promise to his followers: "You will be my witnesses . . . *to the end of the earth*" (Acts 1:8).

Paul likewise spoke confidently of the gospel as being "proclaimed *in all creation under heaven*" (Col. 1:23). And in the heights of the book of Revelation, the apostle John was shown "an eternal gospel to proclaim to those who dwell on earth, to *every nation and tribe and language and people*" (Rev. 14:6); he also heard heavenly beings singing out to Jesus their praise for what he accomplished in the gospel: "you were slain, and by your blood you ransomed people for God *from every tribe and language and people and nation*" (5:9).

All this was envisioned as well in the Old Testament. Paul makes this clear in Romans 15, connecting Christ's purpose with passages such as these from the Psalms: ". . . in order that the Gentiles might glorify God for his mercy. As it is written, 'Therefore I will praise you among the Gentiles'" (Rom. 15:9; citing Ps. 18:49), and "Praise the Lord, all you Gentiles, and let all the peoples extol him" (Rom. 15:11; citing Ps. 117:1). Further, in the messianic prophecy of Psalm 22, David declared, "*All the ends of the earth* shall remember and turn to the LORD, and *all the families of the nations* shall worship before you" (22:27). That's why, through the prophet Isaiah, the Lord of all compassion still cries out everywhere to every human being in history: "Turn to me and be saved, *all the ends of the earth*! For I am God, and there is no other" (Isa. 45:22).

Because Jesus is Lord over *all* things and *all* people everywhere, his gospel could not be more relevant!

NO ONE RIGHTEOUS

The gospel has the power to bring humility among and between the races and ethnicities because it fosters a universal awareness of sin. As awakened urbanites, our humility is critical to our following God in the area of ethnicity.

Yet we easily recognize that although Christ is now and forever Lord over all, *sin* actually reigns over most people's lives. Unless an individual has been reborn by faith in the gospel of Jesus, sin holds sway over him or her, clearly in control. In our natural state, sin—not Christ—is lord of all.

In Romans, Paul goes through an extended argument to show that every single person in the world is sold as a slave to sin. By the time we reach the third chapter of this letter, we hear a devastating assessment from him, expressed in words gleaned from Old Testament truth:

as it is written:

> "None is righteous, no, not one;
>   no one understands;
>   no one seeks for God.
> *All* have turned aside; together they have become worthless;
>   no one does good,
>   not even one." (Rom. 3:10–12)

Yes, there is only one Lord and King—but we refuse to truly serve him. Humanity's massive problem is that none of us obeys our Master and Creator. "For there is no distinction: for all have sinned and fall short of the glory of God" (3:22–23).

IDOLATRY'S GRIP

Back in chapter 1 of Romans, Paul had explained at length (1:18–31) how sin is essentially idolatry. Such idolatry is universal; it isn't primarily a Caucasian problem, an African-American problem, an Asian problem, a Latino problem, or a problem of the uncultured or the underprivileged. The sin of idolatry is a *human* problem that assaults every single person. And the good news of Jesus is the only message anywhere that can effectively address it.

Our biggest problem in the world is not racism or racial hostility, but sin. Racial hostility is only a manifestation and a symptom of our basic problem of sin. It is a manifestation of our own idolatries in raising up our ethnicity over someone else's ethnicity. Racism is ethnic idolatry.

You might insist, "But people in *my* race don't have that attitude." And I would answer that every race tends to express its arrogance and feelings of superiority in different ways, in a manner that each one finds more "acceptable." Furthermore, the observation could be made that every race exhibits different patterns of sin. Yet for all of us, it's still self-serving, it's still idolatry, and it's still rebellion against the Lord. Just because your ethnic group doesn't transgress against God in exactly the same way my race does, doesn't make your race any better than mine.

Gospel movements in our racially diverse cities uniquely display the kingship of Jesus as Ruler over everyone—no matter what our cultural, economic, and ethnic background may be. The gospel has universal, culture-crossing relevance . . . simply because Christ is Lord of all and sin has corrupted all and therefore all need the gospel. The gospel is not a white man's religion, and never has been.

"There is no distinction," Paul had said (Rom. 3:22). There's not one way of salvation for one ethnic or religious group, and some other way for another group. No, there's only *one way* for all people. Many modern people say all religions lead to the same place. But the Bible disagrees with that. In the Bible, God in his goodness points us to a very particular understanding of him and of his risen Son, Jesus, and of our justification by faith alone in him alone.

Jesus "himself is our peace," the gospel declares, and he "has broken down in his flesh the dividing wall of hostility" (Eph. 2:14). All this is accomplished "by the blood of Christ" (2:13). Therefore in Christ we are "no longer strangers and aliens" (2:19); instead, in Christ all believers "are being built *together* into a dwelling place for God by the Spirit" (2:22).

The gospel has full power to save absolutely anyone. If Paul came in our day to Chicago or L.A. or New York, he would be out speaking to our modern-day barbarians and modern-day cultural elites alike. Whether speaking to secular Jews or to traditionalist Jews who practice the Passover, his message would be essentially the same—the gospel of Jesus Christ. In every neighborhood, he would bring the same good news—to the gangster and the shop owner, to the elite professional in his high-rise corner office and the homeless person in a secluded alley.

THE NEED FOR FAITH

Because the gospel is relevant to all, it's also *urgent* for all. For every individual, there's an expiration point for the gospel's relevance; the expiration date is the same as the one that will appear on your death certificate. At that point, your next stop is to stand before the King of kings and Lord of lords. For all of us, that day is coming.

How do we do this? By faith.

Regarding the gospel, Paul affirms, "For in it the righteousness of God is revealed from faith for faith, as it is written, 'The righteous shall live by faith'" (Rom. 1:17). Faith in the gospel of Jesus, the Son of God, means that *his* righteousness becomes *our* righteousness. This is "the free gift of righteousness" Paul refers to in Romans 5:17, a gift allowing us to "reign in life through the one man Jesus Christ." *Anyone who believes* can share in this awesome, triumphant, eternally amazing righteousness of God. That's how potent the gospel is!

And it's a power that gives confidence to its messengers. Paul expressed it this way: "I am not ashamed of the gospel" (1:16). We could also express it positively: "I'm confident in the gospel, and boldly courageous for the gospel, because it is God's power for salvation to everyone who believes."

WHERE ALL THIS IS HEADED

In Revelation 7:9–10, the Lord gave his servant John another glimpse of where the gospel is going:

> After this I looked, and behold, a great multitude that no one could number, from every nation, from all tribes and peoples and languages, standing before the throne and before the Lamb, clothed in white robes, with palm branches in their hands, and crying out with a loud voice, "Salvation belongs to our God who sits on the throne, and to the Lamb!" (Rev. 7:9–10)

It's a beautiful picture of the people who have been changed by the power of the gospel. It's what Paul calls "the obedience of faith . . . among all the nations" (Rom. 1:5). Will we keep that picture close to heart, engraved on our consciousness? Will we see, with true spiritual instinct, that the gospel has relevance and urgency and power for all people—for all ethnicities? Will we place full hope in the gospel as the simple solution to all our complex problems—including the problem of race?

Paul has given us the right example. He wasn't color-blind; he recognized racial and cultural differences. But he courageously and intentionally built relationships across those barriers. He established multiethnic missionary teams and founded multiethnic churches, giving us a worthy ministry model.

God is calling us to see cultural differences as Paul did, while bridging them with the gospel. On a very practical level, we must cultivate relationships with people of every background. If we want diverse churches, we must have diverse relationships.

One of my African-American friends in Chicago used to tell me that if he and I went into black neighborhoods to share the gospel together, the residents would immediately think we were police. Why? Because in racially hostile neighborhoods, two males—one black and one white—just don't hang out. They don't ride in the same car together or stand on a corner together. But if Christians took the lead in building cross-cultural friendships, such a sight would no longer be uncommon.

If you want a diverse church . . . do you have diverse relationships? Is your dinner table or your lunch table diverse? Cultivate diversity personally.

And be personally courageous. Allow the gospel to direct how you view people and treat people and speak to people, even as you allow it to continue working deeper into your life personally. Let others in your world know about their only real hope; let them know the mission you're on.

CONCLUSION

Cities are places of intense diversity, and they're wonderful places to live once we see how the gospel is the solution to the hostilities of race. The gospel solves the problems of race and ethnicity not because they're the main issues the gospel addresses, but because these problems are the result of sin—for which the gospel is the only cure. The gospel solves the problem of hostile hearts by giving us peace—first, peace with a God of wrath, and then, peace with others. This solution to peace with God allows us to foster peace with others.

Our cities, with their convergence of ethnicity and identity and inequality, become critical platforms for the flag of this unifying gospel, which can radically save all who believe. Romans helps urban Christian communities fully understand how the implications of the gospel can reshape community. God's plan for a new, righteous-by-faith humanity transcends ethnicity . . . creating a new unity of those saved from his wrath.

God's gospel has the power to save—and unite—all who believe.

A CLOSING PRAYER

Father in heaven, thank you for the gospel. Thank you that your gospel does what nothing else on earth can ever do—it obliterates all divisions between people—racial, cultural, and otherwise.

We thank you that Christ has accomplished this victory through his willingness to be the Lamb who was slain to take away the sins of the world. It's his name we want to lift up and praise. We know that it's his name that will be praised in eternity by people from every tribe and language and people and nation, and from all the world's cities.

Put that eternal vision in our minds and burn it into our hearts so we don't lose sight of where we're ultimately going, and so we can live today according to that vision.

In Christ's name we pray,
Amen.

8

CHILDREN IN THE CITY

The children seem to have been forgotten.

WILLIAM STRONG, MAYOR OF NEW YORK CITY, LATE 1890S

As for me and my house,
we will serve the LORD.

JOSHUA 24:15

Among America's urban pastors today, few are as widely respected and influential as Timothy Keller, senior pastor at Manhattan's Redeemer Presbyterian Church. In particular, his many books—including the most recent, *Center Church: Doing Balanced, Gospel-Centered Ministry in your City*[1]—give him a profound impact far outside New York City.

It was in the late 1980s when Tim Keller moved to New York with his wife, Kathy, to begin urban ministry. Kathy Keller remembers how ridiculous at first such a move seemed:

> . . . when Tim first mentioned the idea of us going to Manhattan to plant a church, I reacted by laughing. Take our three wild boys (the victims of below-average parenting, as well as indwelling sin) to the center of a big city? Expose them to varieties of sin that I hoped they wouldn't hear about until, say, their mid-30s? My list of answers to "What is wrong with this picture?" was a long, long one.[2]

But in the decades that followed, Kathy would learn "that the city is a wonderful place to raise children, a place where families can flourish in a way that they may not in the suburbs or the small towns." She adds, "My sons loved the city growing up, and love it even more now, not just New York, but all cities. . . . They love the density of people, the diversity of culture, even the sounds and bustle."

She suggests that "the two main advantages of raising your children in the city are also its two main characteristics—*its darkness and its light.*" The city's darkness allows children to "see sin and its consequences while you are still with them and can help them process it."

There's no shortage of sin and its consequences in the urban scene. But, she adds, there's also lots of light:

> Just as the city showcases the worst of the human heart, it also lifts up the best that human culture has achieved. Art and music, drama, architecture, sports, all are the best that they can be. And when you are attending a church full of younger-than-yourself Christians in these professions, your children have role models they can actually embrace.

Following God in the city means seeing with God's lenses the opportunities and challenges of urban living. But plenty of Christian parents can testify to being fearful and anxious about the thought of raising children in the city. They're not sure at all that the city's influence on their children will prove ultimately to be a positive one.

My wife and I—who have five children spread across a ten-year age range, from the early twenties down—can certainly relate to those doubts and fears. We brought our kids to the city when the oldest was in first grade.

GOD, ARE YOU SURE?

I remember when I first sensed God calling our family to the city. I'd been a youth pastor for five years (eventually totaling seven) in a western Chicago suburb when my wife and I began to sense a kind of call to the city. But I was essentially praying, "Are you sure?" I didn't think I could do it.

A milestone came later when we pulled together some of our high school student leaders for a retreat in Wisconsin. After a powerful time of teaching, worship, and repentance together, I sat with a group of about six of them to reflect and pray. We were asking ourselves this question: *What's the one thing you feel is holding you back from fully surrendering yourself to Christ?* The students answered in different ways.

Then they looked at me. "What about you, Jon?"

I wasn't expecting the question to turn to me. I choked up. I had one son and one daughter at the time, and I had this vision that if I moved to the city, one of them would get shot and die (a very irrational fear). So I shared this with them. "I feel like I'm supposed to move to the city," I confessed, "but I feel like I can't because I'm afraid one of my kids would be killed." At the time, the Chicago Public Schools had been rated the worst in the country, and Chicago violence was constantly in the headlines.

In that instant, a teenage girl who was there became a kind of momentary prophet. She looked at me and said, "You know, Jon, if God takes your son away from you, he'll give him back to you."

I couldn't comprehend this. "What are you talking about?" I asked. "Why would you say that?"

She replied, "That's what happens in the Scriptures, isn't it? When God asks Abraham for Isaac, and Abraham obeys, he gets his son back. When God gave his own Son for us, he brought him back alive." She looked at me with great earnestness and added, "If God takes your son, you'll get him back on the day of resurrection."

I felt freed. I was able to tell God, "I can do this—in your strength and not my own. If you go with us, I can go." Praise God!

And as a testimony of God's faithfulness, I have to say that he has taken amazing care of my children. That to me is a fulfillment of this promise. Along with many other parents, we can testify that the urban experience for our children has been both a challenge—and a joy. It *is* possible to raise kids in the city who will thrive.

Your story will be different from ours. But our experience illustrates how it's the gospel itself—that powerful story of God's willing sacrifice in Jesus—that enables and empowers us to follow Christ. God often challenges us to trust him more deeply and follow him in new, unexpected adventures. For my family, he used my fears about the city to surface the question, Can I trust my children to God? Fortunately, he is trustworthy. For God, our thriving means a deep sense of trust—and moves beyond mere physical safety.

FOR A THRIVING HOME

God's biblical vision is for thriving homes. At the close of Psalm 144, David includes words of prayerful blessing that give us great vision for a thriving home, in the city or anywhere. The blessing begins, "May our sons in their youth be like plants full grown, our daughters like corner pillars cut for the structure of a palace" (Ps. 144:12). These pictures exude the vitality and strength of sons and daughters alike. And yet this vision for children endued with strength is preceded by a sense of *God's* power and a plea for that power to touch our lives: "Bow your heavens, O LORD, and come down! Touch the mountains so that they smoke!" (144:5).

Our concern for our children and our trust in God's strength raise questions for us as we seek to follow God in the urban generation. How, as urban parents, do we pursue such an atmosphere of beauty and vitality in our homes? How do we faithfully raise our children in the city—or anywhere—in such a way that they not only prevail, but thrive?

Interestingly, one of the clearest and most direct teachings in all of Scripture on rightly raising children is found in yet another letter from Paul originally directed to a specifically urban audience—this time to the believers in the great ancient city of Ephesus.[3] In fact, if it were written today, this book of Ephesians might well be called something like "Chicagoans" or "Bostonians" or "Parisians." Wisdom for parenting, counterintuitively to moderns, comes not under some title on raising children effectively, but embedded in a theologically rich book. And its author, Paul, was of course a highly urban individual himself—a lover of cities, a man of the marketplace and the amphitheater.

Of course the wisdom for the Ephesians applies broadly. His message was likely a "circular" letter that was also passed along to other cities and areas in the surrounding region (in what is today western Turkey). Perhaps this epistle has come down to us as addressed particularly to the Ephesians because of Paul's longstanding pastoral relationship with the believers there. Paul had taught night and day in Ephesus for three years (Acts 20:31). Ephesus was by far the largest and most important metropolis in that area. A political, financial, and religious center, Ephesus was also a prosperous crossroad for trade.

The city's strong religious influence was centered upon the worship of the goddess of fertility, whose Greek name was Artemis and whose Latin name was Diana. Her temple in Ephesus was considered one of the seven wonders of the world. Surrounded by 127 columns, each sixty feet high, it was the largest Greek temple ever built and the first to be constructed entirely of marble.[4]

The temple's grandeur reflected the prominence given to the cult of this goddess. The city jealously guarded its prestige as being "temple keeper of the great Artemis, and of the sacred stone that fell from the sky," as an Ephesus city official affirmed in Acts 19:35. The worship of Artemis and veneration of her temple brought in untold wealth to Ephesus from tourists, pilgrims, and cultists.

Artemis, shown in statuary as being multiple-breasted, was the focus of a local prostitution industry in a culture of perverse sexual idolatry.[5] That didn't add up to a very hospitable context for Christian families. With such a corrupting environment, Ephesus sounds to our modern way of thinking like the kind of place Paul would tell Christian parents simply to flee—and the sooner the better. But instead, in his letter he simply focuses on encouraging parents to wisely instruct their children in the Lord.

Such encouragement is found concentrated in the opening verses of Ephesians 6, offering a treasure-trove of principles for how our children can thrive and prevail, by God's intention, even in the city.

THE VISION

Paul's Christ-centered vision for raising children is part of his instructions to the whole household. In the immediately preceding verses in Ephesians, in the last part of chapter 5, Paul had addressed the attitudes and conduct of godly husbands and wives. Now, here in chapter 6, he turns to parents and children, and he lays out a vision for them that springs from the gospel.

We see this as he writes, "Children, obey your parents *in the Lord*, for this is right" (Eph. 6:1). By "in the Lord," he means the Lord Jesus. Paul is reminding us that his words of instruction for families come in the context of the most powerful story ever told, the gospel of the King of kings who reigns over all things, who humbly came to the earth and *became a child* himself. This man lived without sinning, was rejected by his own people, was put to death, and was buried—but then rose again from the dead. He now reigns in triumph over all creation forever. This

One, the Lord Jesus Christ, died for children, for parents, for singles, for married people—that their lives might be utterly transformed.

"In the Lord"—these are priceless words from Paul. They refer to our *union* with Christ. Ephesians is rich with our inseparable connection to a risen Lord. As a believer, every blessing you have comes from your being *in* the Lord Jesus—being connected with him, alive to him through his Spirit. In fact, in his opening words to this letter Paul writes of how God "has *blessed us in Christ with every spiritual blessing* in the heavenly places" (Eph. 1:3). Every single blessing you have—the forgiveness of your sin, your access to a heavenly Father—all this comes from the fact that you are *in Christ*.

So when Paul instructs children here to obey their parents, don't miss that phrase immediately following: "in the Lord." In the gospel, children's obedience to parents reflects a love for a higher authority, a higher King. This is discipleship. One biblical scholar puts it this way: "The obedience of Christian children to their parents is all of a piece with their submission to Christ."[6] And "in the Lord" defines the scope of obedience. Parents do not always do what is right or instruct correctly. Children look to their parents and see beyond to the risen Christ.

This principle also means that if you're a child having trouble obeying your parents, or a parent having trouble with a rebellious child, the solution isn't simply to try harder. The solution is to go back to the truth of the risen Lord who sacrificed himself on your behalf, and to keep reflecting on what this really means for us. You let it saturate your mind and heart. It means continually developing a deeper understanding and appreciation for Jesus and his gospel.

That's the vision Paul is pushing. Christian parenting is not primarily about bedtimes or chores, but about the fundamental truth of the gospel. After all, Paul is addressing godly marriages and godly families in just a few paragraphs here, after first spending three chapters spelling out the deep truths of the gospel and our blessings in Christ—and then two more chapters on the wider implications of these blessings. That's where the power really comes from.

Paul's entire perspective on what it takes to raise children well is inseparable from this vision of a resurrected and risen Lord who was crucified on our behalf, and who now is reigning over all things. The gospel helps us parent. The gospel helps us obey. This forms the foundation for raising children who thrive and prevail. It's built on fundamental truths about God and about each of us that Paul spells out earlier in this letter:

> . . . you were dead in the trespasses and sins . . . and were by nature children of wrath, like the rest of mankind. *But God*, being rich in mercy, because of the great love with which he loved us, even when we were dead in our trespasses, made us alive together with Christ. (Eph. 2:1, 3–5)

Every parent and child has been in rebellion against God, but *God has done something decisive* about that. He's given us an entirely new life *in Christ*.

THE FABRIC

While the in-Christ vision is essential, another principle is present in these words from Paul. We can picture it as the *fabric* of raising children who thrive and prevail in the city. Look again at what Paul says here, and notice the imperative verbs he uses:

> Children, *obey* your parents in the Lord, for this is right. "*Honor* your father and mother" (this is the first commandment with a promise), "that it may go well with you and that you may live long in the land." (Eph. 6:1–3)

This fabric for the family is woven of obedience and honor. They go together. Paul's logic for obedience in the Lord is common sense: "this is right." Hard to argue with that. In a somewhat parallel passage in his letter to Colossians, Paul writes, "Children, obey your parents in everything, for *this pleases the Lord*" (Col. 3:20). Pleasing the Lord is always *right*, and children do this when obeying their parents from the heart.

But Paul buttresses his argument for obedience (here in Ephesians 6) by quoting the Old Testament. He turns to the fifth of the Ten Commandments, reinforcing the rightness and goodness of such obedience. We're to honor father and mother, and this brings us benefit (more on this to follow).

Those two words *obey* and *honor* belong together, because they're not exactly the same thing yet they are very complementary. *Obedience* involves the outward submission to parents, through actions. But notice, you can obey without honoring, by doing the correct outward actions but with the wrong motive or attitude. *Honor* has to do with an attitude, and a view of joy and thankfulness as obedience is carried out. You may have heard the story of the four-year-old boy who, standing defiantly, is told to sit down at the dinner table. When he finally obeys and sits down, he lets his parents know, "I'm still standing up on the inside!"

Honor involves outward obedience, but it also involves the heart attitude of kindness. The Hebrew meaning of the words literally corresponds to showing the weightiness of another, his or her worth and value. Children can show this through their actions and words. Think for instance of a child's respectful words, "Okay, Mom!" when asked to do the simple daily things—make a bed or set a table—but think also of a kind compliment, a scribbled thank-you note or card, or the gift of a hand-drawn picture hung on the fridge. Thoughtfulness shows a heart attitude.

When both obedience and honor are present in a home, they sound forth a compelling message all around. They show the kind of gospel-changed lives that are needed right at the heart of our cities. Think about this from the perspective of early Christianity as a movement. How did the gospel continue to grow as rapidly as it did throughout the Roman empire? It exploded through the growth and multiplication of tiny cells—*godly homes* which became little house churches, where Christ was exalted, where minds and hearts were saturated in God's Word, and where parents were honored and obeyed. Building godly families and homes was a part of what God used to infiltrate and change cities and regions beyond with the gospel.

THE PROMISE OF LIFE

There's a promise in this passage as well, as Paul emphasizes, for those who want to follow God faithfully. When our children obey through the gospel and honor their mother and father, they indeed thrive: things "go well" with them, that they may "live long in the land" (Eph. 6:1).

This is a striking promise. It's included in the original fifth commandment, which Paul is quoting here: "Honor your father and your mother, that your days may be long in the land that the LORD your God is giving you" (Ex. 20:12). The sentiment is that those who live in the fear of God, and who reflect it in their relationships, will outlive others. This theme shows up often in wisdom literature, which speaks of the benefits of godliness, including long days. In Psalm 91:15–16 we hear God say of the faithful believer, "When he calls to me, I will answer him; I will be with him in trouble. . . . *With long life I will satisfy him* and show him my salvation." And Proverbs 3, depicting wisdom as a woman, tells us, "Long life is in her right hand; in her left hand are riches and honor" (Prov. 3:16). Earlier we read, "My son, do not forget my teaching, but let your heart keep my commandments, for *length of days and years of life* and peace they will add to you" (3:1–2). Proverbs throughout envisions children clinging to the wisdom of their parents and receiving the fruit of longevity.

Paul isn't making an iron-clad guarantee that every submissive child will automatically live into his or her nineties. In the broadest understanding of this Old Testament imagery, this promise points to the truly good life of *shalom*, which reaches its full and final completion of *eternal* life in God's presence.

Before we move on to the next section, I want to spend some time on one particular implication related to the fabric of obedience for raising children who thrive in the city. The pattern Paul weaves together for us is one of *vitally engaged* parents. If our children are honoring and obeying their parents to the point that they're holding deeply to our teaching—well then, these godly, gospel-teaching parents are *involved*; the children have someone to obey and honor. In other words, the parents are *present*.

The promise to "live long in the land" is made in the context of godly, nurturing families. From the biblical perspective of wisdom literature, godly instruction handed down from generation to generation is God's intention. Some have written recently about the concept of the "Mozart effect," which has to do not with how much music one hears at an early age, but with the critical importance of *fathers* being involved in their children's lives.[7] The idea is that a father who invests in his children will instill a confidence in them that allows them to thrive in a way they otherwise would not. The term comes from the pattern seen in the life of Mozart, whose father scrupulously assisted his development in every aspect.

In Paul's thought, this promise for his readers to "live long in the land" has nothing to do with geographic location—urban or rural. It has to do with *obedience*. The solution for longevity isn't to depart our cities and escape their problems, but rather to focus on raising godly families *right where we are*. I sense that Paul is pushing for the stability and longevity of our children here in their urban locale as the correct context for their faithfulness to the Lord, their faithfulness to each other, and their faithfulness to their community.

One of the most difficult problems in cities around the world, and particularly in North America, is that of broken families. I'm not saying I have the answers for it; I'm saying the severity of it should wake us up.

A number of years ago, after being in the city for some time, I stumbled on a haunting urban phrase. When talking with a friend named Theo, who had grown up in one of Chicago's roughest neighborhoods, I asked him the age of one of his friends. He responded, "He just made eighteen."

Puzzled by this curious expression, I asked what he meant by "just made."

Theo pointed out that "made" was an accomplishment. He mentioned how eight of the friends he'd grown up with had been killed one way or another over the years. In that environment, his friend hadn't "turned" eighteen; he had *made* it there.

Theo also told me that almost none of his friends had known their fathers. Which means they'd never had the opportunity to have a godly father whom they could obey, let alone honor or imitate. I'm not saying fatherlessness is somehow fatal; it isn't. God is the Father of the fatherless. But certainly the lives of Theo's friends would have been different if they'd had an earthly, godly father to honor.

Our cities need godly, gospel families.

THE WARNING TO FATHERS

Into the mix here in Ephesians 6, Paul adds directives specifically for dads. "Fathers," he writes, "do not provoke your children to anger, but bring them up in the discipline and instruction of the Lord" (Eph. 6:4).

Paul amplifies this in a corresponding passage in his letter to the Colossian believers: "Fathers, do not provoke your children, lest they become discouraged" (Col. 3:21). In these short phrases, Paul gives both guidance and a warning for fathers. Their role in raising children who will thrive and prevail in the city is to be one of gentleness, not of prodding and provocation.

Children are delicate. God has fashioned each one with a unique personality that he intends for parents to nurture so that child flourishes. Fathers are not wrecking balls. We can use our parental authority to irritate, antagonize, goad, and inflame a child. But we must not.

"No," Paul says to dads, "you don't lead your kids that way."

With five children of my own, I know I have to be very careful in how I nurture and cultivate each one. Paul is saying, "Dads, intervene. Be lovingly involved. It's your responsibility. Take time to raise your own children. Discipline them, yes—but with gentleness and encouragement." That's our guidance.

I've encountered some funny reactions when I'm out in public with my children. "Are all those *yours*?" is a typical reaction. I remember being in a park with my kids a number of years ago, and someone asked me, "On duty today?" As if I'm just a guy providing childcare. I wanted to say, "No! This is *my* privilege! I'm a dad. I'm *supposed* to be with my kids." But in a culture where Dad is so often absent, a father with five kids in tow can be a strange sight. Dads don't just "do childcare." They're *dads*.

PARENTING AS THE SCHOOL OF DISCIPLESHIP

When Paul speaks positively of how fathers—and, by implication, mothers—are to raise their children, he uses two primary ideas. He tells them to bring up their children "in the *discipline* and *instruction* of the Lord" (Eph. 6:4).

The idea of "discipline" might seem exclusively related to punishment. But it's a more robust term. It's from the Greek *paideia*, which literally means the act of providing guidance for responsible living.[8] It's closely aligned with a kind of far-reaching tutoring, providing a pathway of development. Paul has in mind the sort of comprehensive life-training that brings a child all the way into maturity.

The whole arrangement of the Christian household is to *instruct*. This is discipleship. It involves clearly showing the way, envisioning a child's future on a path of righteousness made possible by the gospel—a future filled with the adventure of following the Lord.

Imagine a parent reading to a child, then later helping her choose what to read, then later asking what she's reading—that's a picture of the development. It involves helping our children know Christ, grasp the Scriptures, and learn to make gospel-centered choices.

Paul's second term, "instruction" (sometimes translated "admonishment"), refers primarily to verbal teaching rather than the total environment or pathway of discipleship. Here parents must instill the content of Christian teaching, using necessary words of encouragement and correction along the way.

These two ideas—the pathway of discipleship and the content of Christian teaching—comprise the whole package for raising children. This requires *active* parenting, not passive. Paul says, "Bring them up . . ." That's the language of determined and directed involvement, of taking responsibility. If parents aren't at work to keep their children on the right path, they're showing that they don't really love them. Disengaged parents are not loving their children.

Another way to think of it is this: *the gospel-centered family is itself a school.* We raise our children in a daily classroom that focuses on "the discipline and instruction *of the Lord.*" We focus on the risen Christ. Our vision is for our children to thrive and prevail under *his* care and authority. That's what helps them thrive and prevail. It doesn't matter whether we have our children in a public school, a private school, or home school—the gospel must be at the core of our instruction and training as a parent.

In fact, regardless of where your children are formally educated, the family itself is always a school—the school of life. Parental responsibility in the home to bring up children in the Lord's instruction and training and wisdom must always be the foundation for a child's development. The home is meant to be a place where children learn to pray, where they learn to read the Scriptures, where they express the joy of "singing psalms and hymns and spiritual songs" (Col. 3:16).

The American dream promotes an unrelenting concentration on

preparing children to secure their material and physical and emotional well-being. The gospel tells us something different, something bigger and better; the gospel guides parents to instill in the children a love for the beauty of the resurrected Lord as the One who is reigning over all things.

That's the key to nurturing and instructing children in the city.

A CLOSING PRAYER

Father, thank you that you have been a Father to us, caring and providing for us. Thank you also for offering your own Son, who was crucified for our sins. And thank you for the sons and daughters you continue to give to our families, and our calling to raise them up in a way that's fully centered on you.

Whether we are married or single, young or old, our desire is to live in whole-hearted devotion to you in our cities and elsewhere. And we pray for the coming generation of believers, that they will give themselves unreservedly to you, since you gave yourself unreservedly for us to be our Redeemer.

We praise you for this, in Christ's name,
Amen.

PART 4

STRATEGIC PRINCIPLES AND ACTIONS

Reaching the City

So the word of the Lord continued to increase and prevail mightily.

ACTS 19:20

9

THE CITY
WITHIN A CITY

The bright lights of the city's center at night have always
beckoned to the young and adventurous. . . .
To this day, lights of a city—
seen approaching from land, sea, or air—
signify the warmth and buzz of human activity,
against the surrounding darkness.

IRVING LEWIS ALLEN

Arise, shine, for your light has come,
and the glory of the LORD *has risen upon you.*
For behold, darkness shall cover the earth,
and thick darkness the peoples;
but the LORD *will arise upon you,*
and his glory will be seen upon you.
And nations shall come to your light.

ISAIAH 60:1-3

The most important city in the world is not New York with its financial
clout, or Washington with its political muscle, or Paris for setting the
latest standard in food and fashion, or Shanghai or Mumbai or Dubai for
racing ahead in economic growth, or Los Angeles or London for shaping
pop culture around the globe.

It's none of those. The most important city in the world is simply
God's people. In every locale, they're a "city within the city." They represent an enduring city, one that will outlast every other city.

That's the perspective coming through in some stunning words spoken by Jesus.

CITY OF LIGHT, CITY ON A HILL

Here's the passage. It's a familiar one, but imagine hearing these things for the very first time:

> You are the light of the world. A city set on a hill cannot be hidden. Nor do people light a lamp and put it under a basket, but on a stand, and it gives light to all in the house. (Matt. 5:14–15)

What a description: *the light of the world*! Here is the striking truth: God's plan to illuminate the world—including our cities—with the gospel is borne by humble, ordinary people. God's church shines with an eternal, life-giving light! No matter if it's a storefront congregation of thirty, a suburban congregation of a thousand, or a rural congregation of thirty-nine, the light is the same: *Christ*. This source of *our* light gives us energy for our mission. And all the world needs the light of Christ.

We know that Jesus spoke in these terms in a different place and time—when he was actually referring to *himself*, not to his followers. Standing in Jerusalem's temple he announced, "*I* am the light of the world. Whoever follows me will not walk in darkness, but will have the light of life" (John 8:12).

But here on the Galilean hillside, as described in the Gospel of Matthew, as Jesus gives the Sermon on the Mount—the greatest sermon ever preached—he tells his followers, "*You* are the light of the world" (Matt. 5:14). And that "you" is indeed emphatic. Jesus confronts his disciples with the amazing fact that they're like a city topping a lofty slope in unobstructed sight, or like a blazing lamp placed high upon a stand, filling an entire room with its brilliance.

No matter where we live, these words from Jesus represent our call to realize the radiant identity we have in our connection to Christ, because of the divine life and power flowing within and through us. We thus have a powerful and desperately needed role today in a world wrapped in darkness.

Martyn Lloyd-Jones, who preached for three decades in twentieth-century London, could see the marvel in these words from Jesus. When he gave a sermon on this passage, he pointed to what it offers us:

We have, surely, one of the most astounding and extraordinary statements about the Christian that was ever made, even by our Lord and Savior Jesus Christ Himself. When you consider the setting, and remember the people to whom our Lord uttered these words, they do indeed become most remarkable. It is a statement full of significance and profound implications with regard to an understanding of the nature of the Christian life . . . one of those statements which should always have the effect upon us of making us lift up our heads, causing us to realize once more what a remarkable and glorious thing it is to be a Christian.[1]

You may not always feel that being a Christian is such "a remarkable and glorious thing," especially on that Monday morning before coffee when you drag yourself out of bed, or a late Friday night when a teenager has not returned home—but that's exactly the takeaway from this passage that Jesus wants you to receive. It's the same response he sought from those in Galilee who first heard these words. To all who would follow him, whether the brawny fisherman like Peter, or the freshly healed paralytic in the crowd, the Lord points to these striking images of light and says, "*This* is your new identity, if you are in me."

Jesus invites us to see ourselves as a city on a hill and a city of light, with full understanding of all that this means. He's giving his disciples a blueprint for gospel-change: his people are torchbearers of the truth in a darkened world.

Paris has often been called the City of Light, with the illuminated Eiffel Tower shimmering at night, and the River Seine reflecting streetlights. But it's an illusion; the true City of Light is the people of God.

It means we have a new identity. God doesn't tell us *to be* the light; he says *we are* the light. That's the real distinction of all who are in Christ. We're a city of light within a city of darkness. In Paris, Shanghai, Cairo, and all the great cities of the world—as well as among the vast numbers of unreached people scattered far from cities—every person desperately needs the illumination of the gospel that only the church carries.

COMMON PEOPLE, BEARERS OF LIGHT

The people who first heard these words from Jesus were not some distinguished assembly of movers and shakers, personages of royalty or rank or fame, men or women of great wealth or intellect or accomplishment. Instead, his listeners that day were conspicuous only for their commonness.

We can see this when we explore the setting for this passage, back in the verses leading up to the Sermon on the Mount. Look at the evidence for what kinds of people would have been present on that occasion to hear Jesus teach:

> . . . and they brought him all the sick, those afflicted with various diseases and pains, those oppressed by demons, epileptics, and paralytics, and he healed them. And great crowds followed him from Galilee and the Decapolis, and from Jerusalem and Judea, and from beyond the Jordan. Seeing the crowds, he went up on the mountain, and when he sat down, his disciples came to him. And he opened his mouth and taught them . . . (Matt. 4:24–5:2)

The "disciples" mentioned here would include four simple, hard-working fishermen. Jesus had just called Peter, Andrew, James, and John to leave everything—their fathers, nets, boats—to follow him and become fishers of men (Matt. 4:18–22). Pressing in behind the likes of these guys on the hillside on this day was a larger crowd of interested folks, in these early days of the growing fame of Jesus. This crowd includes the least, the lowest, and the overlooked. Lloyd-Jones describes the crowd as "those simple people, those entirely unimportant people from the standpoint of the world." But from the standpoint of Jesus, they were the carriers of this dark world's only true light.

This is an identity we all share *collectively* as believers. When Jesus said, "You are the light of the world," this *you* in the Greek language is plural—meaning "all of you." Light-bearing is not an individual project. Following Christ in our urban generation is done *together*. Just as the first-century church met in the temple and from house to house (Acts 5:42), Christians in our cities *must* gather regularly (Acts 2:46; 20:20; Heb. 10:24–25). Elsewhere the Scriptures refer to the Lord's people as "one body" (Rom. 12:4–5; 1 Cor. 12:12; Eph. 4:4).

Jesus is expressing our new corporate identity: *Together, all of you are the light of the world.* Jesus does not envision a single candle shining bravely in the dark night; no, we're to shine radiantly as thousands and thousands of candles together, like the twinkling lights of a city that crowns a hilltop. The church gathered *matters*.

It's very easy in the press and busyness of urban living or the isolation of city culture to succumb to "urban drift"—a movement away from relationship, away from the burden-bearing, supportive, illuminating community of Christ. But it's among God's people, as we gather around his light-giving Word, that the flames of our faith are renewed.

Do you comprehend why our cities and the ends of the earth so desperately need the light of the gospel held high by his people? Be honest: are you fully "in" as a part of this overall community project that is imaging God to the world?

A REFLECTION OF TRUE LIGHT

Jesus wraps up this "light" passage with these words:

> In the same way, let your light shine before others, so that they may see your good works *and give glory to your Father who is in heaven*. (Matt. 5:16)

As disciples of Jesus, we do not exist for ourselves. The church exists for the glory and fame of God—at the center of the city and to the ends of the earth. Jesus authoritatively commands us to let our light shine so others will ultimately glorify God. We radiate the identity of Christ when we witness to the work of Christ and carry out the deeds of Christ.

Our function and role—our calling and purpose—is very simple. It is to bring eternal glory to the Father. As an individual Christian, you are to fully participate in this cosmic and eternal community, the people of God, that *constantly glorifies God*.

That's why you exist. If you're in the city, that's *why* you're in the city. If you're under the massive skies of Montana, or along the rocky coasts of Maine, or in the sprawling slums of Mumbai, that's *why* you're there. Your existence and mine was never really about us in the first place, and it isn't about us even now. Our lives are not primarily about our jobs or vocation, or anything else we're doing or pursuing. Those things may be important, but ultimately the point of our life must be about *him*, with our "light" directed ultimately and exclusively to him. We reflect him. Montana, Maine, and Mumbai all need a light—and his church, his people, are that light.

That's a higher calling for us than finding a spouse, or launching a great career, or accomplishing whatever dreams we might have. Life's overarching purpose is the radiance and outshining and glory of God. And this happens, according to Matthew 5:16, through our *witness* and *good works*—all that the Spirit of God and the grace of God will empower and direct us to *do* in serving God and people. God's glory is why we shine.

THE LIGHT WITHIN

But if God's glory is the reason we shine, then we must also be clear on *how* we shine. In this shining city whose image Jesus puts into our minds and hearts, the light emanates from him and reflects his own light.

You and I shine only because Christ—the light of the world—shines within us. *We* are not the power source; the Son of God is. He's the One who illumines his people, and they then shine in the world and illumine others as well. As the world sees this light, which is actually emanating from Jesus, they're attracted to it, which then brings glory to the Father.

Lloyd-Jones expressed it this way:

> As those who believe the gospel we have received light and knowledge and instruction. *But,* in addition, it has become part of us. It has become our life, so that we thus become reflectors of it. The remarkable thing, therefore, of which we are reminded here is our intimate relationship with Him. The Christian is a man who has received and has become a partaker of the divine nature. The light that is Christ Himself, the light that is ultimately God, is the light that is in the Christian.[2]

So it is that the church, in the city or beyond, must find its total identity in Jesus, in the message of the death and resurrection of Christ and his Spirit-empowering to be light in the world. When the church drifts from Christ, we drift from the light. Therefore our first project in city-change is really *personal change*—knowing Christ through the gospel.

How are you doing in remembering, dwelling in, and enjoying the *source* of your light? Paul tells us that "God, who said, 'Let light shine out of darkness,' has shone in our hearts to give the light of the knowledge of the glory of God in the face of Jesus Christ" (2 Cor. 4:6). Are you reflecting Christ? It's *his* light and *his* power, so if you feel you're fading, the problem is your connection to the Light, to the One who illumines.

Particularly in sprawling, unevangelized cities, it's often easy to feel the darkness and dirtiness, and to even be overwhelmed by it. Perhaps we try to overlook the spiritual darkness by focusing instead on the brilliant neon, on the city's vibrancy and life and energy. But even when we sense an oppressive spiritual shadow over everything, Jesus tells us that within that setting, Christians themselves are a separate city, shining there *for* him and *to* him—and we do it in order to glorify the God of light. That's our calling in such a place.

THE STORY OF LIGHT

Physically, there's so much light around us that it's easy to simply take it for granted and fail to appreciate all that light makes possible for us. Can you even begin to imagine what our world would be like without any light?

So it's really no little thing that the Lord calls us "light." Just as he lets physical light play such a huge role in our earthly existence and surroundings, so also the image of light has a vast and preeminent presence in Scripture, from beginning to end. To impress more deeply on us our amazing privilege as light-bearers, we should dwell here for a moment. Reading with our eyes wide open, we can detect a logical progression, a beautiful wholeness, and a strong relational connection in all the classic "light" passages of Scripture.

We see that "*God is light*, and in him is no darkness at all" (1 John 1:5). We remember that, in the beginning, "God said, '*Let there be light*,' and there was light" (Gen. 1:3). The God of light himself gave us a world of light in every way—until mankind's sin plunged us into a gloom we couldn't shake.

Still, God extended a glimmer of promise our way: "because of the tender mercy of our God, . . . the sunrise shall visit us from on high to give *light* to those who sit in darkness and in the shadow of death" (Luke 1:78–79). He tells us of a new dawn.

And sure enough, Jesus burst on the scene in a blaze of unsurpassed glory. As God in human flesh, he announced, "*I am the light of the world*"

(John 8:12). Ancient prophecy is now fulfilled: "the people dwelling in darkness have seen a great light, and for those dwelling in the region and shadow of death, on them a light has dawned" (Matt. 4:16).

This shining One came to us overflowing with life, "and the life was the *light* of men" (John 1:4). As he removes our sin and its blanket of darkness through his own death and resurrection, Jesus instills his rays within us. By true faith we're so linked with him and alive in him that Jesus, who is *the* light of the world, calls *us* to shine as *the* light of the world, just as we've seen in Matthew 5. That light is our God-given heat and energy and illumination, always revealing itself as being divine, always reflecting back upon the Father. *We* shine so that *he* can shine more.

What an honor! It means an identity greater than anything else possible on earth, for the Lord tells us, "now you are *light in the Lord*. Walk as *children of light*" (Eph. 5:8). It also means a joyful new purpose and privilege: to "proclaim the excellencies of him who called you out of darkness into his marvelous light" (1 Pet. 2:9). These "excellencies" of God are brilliantly clarified for us by God's Spirit and his Word and his grace. And then, so that others can see these things about God, they're lit up by our own lives that keep drawing attention to the Source.

All this precious light is fully *ours*, to receive and reflect. Therefore each of us can declare, "The LORD is *my light* and my salvation; whom shall I fear?" (Ps. 27:1). Day by day, moment by moment, each of us can say to him with gratitude, "Your word is a *lamp to my feet* and a *light to my path*" (Ps. 119:105).

*And yet—somehow—*not everyone will accept what the God of light has done for us. Many prefer to remain rebels at heart; many are so enslaved to sin's darkness that they cringe before the light: "And this is the judgment: the *light* has come into the world, and *people loved the darkness* rather than the light because their works were evil. For everyone who does wicked things hates the light and does not come to the light, lest his works should be exposed" (John 3:19–20). Paul tells us that some have their eyes veiled: "And even if our gospel is veiled, it is veiled to those who are perishing. In their case the god of this world has blinded the minds of the unbelievers, to keep them from seeing the light of the gospel of the glory of Christ, who is the image of God" (2 Cor. 4:3–4).

So that's the situation. As believers, awakened urbanites and non-urbanites, we're light-bearers in a world still drowning in darkness. The Lord tells us he has temporarily left us here in this murky and corrupt world as righteous beacons for a sea of lost souls, "among whom you *shine* as *lights* in the world" (Phil. 2:15). For this moment, this is our mission. Put differently, your neighborhood—your neighbors—need *you* to shine the light of Christ to them. You hold a torch of the gospel for them.

Seeing our light, as we continue to let it blaze, some will believe, and some will not. But, as Jesus promised, those who *do* believe will give glory to our Father who is in heaven. The focus ultimately will always come back to him.

Then at last the time will come when we're taken up into the everlasting light of the new city, the New Jerusalem, which "has no need of sun or moon to shine on it, for *the glory of God gives it light*, and *its lamp is the Lamb*. By its light will the nations walk, . . . and there will be no night there" (Rev. 21:23–25). In such a brilliant atmosphere of pure light and nightless glory, we'll find unimaginable fulfillment and satisfaction that never fades but only keeps expanding in new dimensions that we can't begin to fathom here and now.

This is good news—particularly for those who've wondered what's beyond this life and this world—and who now see Christ as the light.

LIGHT INCLUDES HOLINESS

In the Scriptures, blinding light is very often associated with God's revealing of himself. God's holiness is intricately linked with light. Light as a spiritual concept includes holiness—for God, *and* for us. This is also behind what Jesus means by the city of light and the city on a hill.

As light-bearers, as a community of light, we're called together to live this life of holiness. Our cities need to see this vision of holiness.

Steve Timmis is a British pastor and church planter, as well as coauthor of *Total Church: A Radical Reshaping around Gospel and Community*. "Holiness," he writes, "is not less than an individual Christian living distinctively." He then adds that "holiness is a community project," since "it is together that we image God."[3] It takes all of us to shine with Christ's holy light as the light of the world.

In a practical and sensible way, Paul dwells extensively on the dynamics of this light-versus-darkness holiness in his letter to the urban believers in Ephesus. A passage near the letter's end (in 5:7–14) is saturated with this imagery and gives sound instruction for today's urban believers. Paul first reminds the Ephesians, "at one time you were *darkness*" (v. 8)—something that has been true of all of us today. It's not that we were simply living in darkness; we actually *were* darkness—darkness was our identity, our essence.

"But now," Paul continues, "you are *light* in the Lord" (Eph. 5:8). Through the gospel, our identity and essence are radically transformed, in the most comprehensive change imaginable.

Such a new level of existence—our high calling to *be* light—brings with it obligation:

> *Walk as children of light* (for the fruit of light is found *in all that is good and right and true*), and *try to discern what is pleasing to the Lord.* (Eph. 5:8–10)

As they continue living in the morally corrupt atmosphere that pervaded contemporary Ephesus, Paul tells his readers,

> Take no part in the unfruitful works of darkness, but instead expose them. For it is shameful even to speak of the things that they do in secret. (Eph. 5:11–12)

This is wise and practical counsel. When confronted with choices in the dense and diverse urban setting, when we wonder if we should participate in something, we can simply ask: "Is this an activity of those who walk in the light, or of those who walk in the darkness?"

In that context, Paul is struck especially by the inherent *power* of light:

> But when anything is exposed by the light, it becomes visible, for anything that becomes visible *is* light. (Eph. 5:13–14)

Paul is reminded here of Old Testament truth that takes on a new life with the coming of Christ:

Therefore it says,

> "Awake, O sleeper,
>   and arise from the dead,
>   and *Christ will shine on you*." (v. 14)

Living out the light is like a morning-fresh awakening, a sharing in the resurrection power of Jesus, and a bathing in the glow of all that Christ himself is and owns.

That glow was apparent to a young woman named Ming-Un.

She came to our community in Chicago for only a few months at the end of one summer, speaking little English, yet eager to learn American culture. When one family in our church adopted her into their home, she saw the gospel's light firsthand around their dinner table. When invited into community with other believers, taking time away on vacation with Christians, she again heard and saw the gospel lived out.

Only three weeks before returning to Shanghai, she showed up one Sunday at church to say, "I became a Christian on Wednesday." What made the difference? The light of the gospel of Jesus in the family life she witnessed among us in Chicago. To God be the glory.

A LIGHT THAT'S HATED

Light has a purpose, which is to shine and to reveal. And since we're given an intimate sharing in the light of Christ, we also share in the same kind of reaction that he received. This is spelled out for us in John 3:19–21, which explains the rejection and hatred of Jesus that eventually led to his death:

> the light has come into the world, and people loved the darkness rather than the light because their works were evil. For everyone who does wicked things hates the light and does not come to the light, lest his works should be exposed. But whoever does what is true comes to the light, so that it may be clearly seen that his works have been carried out in God. (John 3:19–21)

157

Here the words of Lloyd-Jones are again helpful:

> What is the effect of light? What does it really do? There can be no doubt that the first thing light does is to expose the darkness and the things that belong to darkness.[4]

As we shine our Christ-given light, we can expect, like Jesus, to receive rejection and hatred from those in this world who are sold out to evil.

In the Sermon of the Mount, before calling his disciples "the light of the world," Jesus had first warned them of persecution—and of the privilege of enduring this treatment for his sake:

> Blessed are you when others revile you and persecute you and utter all kinds of evil against you falsely on my account. Rejoice and be glad, for your reward is great in heaven, for so they persecuted the prophets who were before you. (Matt. 5:11–12)

As light-bearers in a world that still obeys the darkness, our life won't be easy or simple. We can expect hostility from others. But we will be rewarded for having an illuminating effect.

God's church preaching God's gospel is God's strategy for change in our world. The greatest need of our cities, many of which are less than one percent gospel-believing, is the renewing light of the gospel.

LIVING THE LIGHT

How do we put all this into practice? How do we see God's people shine with the light that our cities so desperately need?

First, we recognize that we cannot shine any light without Christ, who is ultimately the only light of the world. He is the source. We cannot *be* light unless we *have* the light. Our initial step in shining Christ's light into the world is to ensure that we've received his light by faith. This requires coming to Christ as the light of the world and repenting of our own darkness.

How? We look to the cross, where the light of the world was extinguished, his life snuffed out, with the lifeless body of Christ carried off to be buried in a dark tomb. We remember that he was raised from the dead in everlasting light, forever proving his victory over the darkness and death of sin. We thank him that every human being has the opportunity to repent of sin and of walking in darkness. We trust him to transfer us from the kingdom of darkness to the kingdom of light. We receive God's forgiveness, and walk freely in the light.

Second, we ensure that we're living out the gospel in the local church and in our neighborhoods. Are we with Gods' people? Are we repenting of known sins? Are we walking in the light? Jesus has been telling us, "You have an illuminating power within you which must never be blocked or shrouded; it's intended to shine forth." As the world's light, we must be out there in the dark world, spending time with those who don't know Jesus and haven't understood or appreciated his light. Cultivate those relationships. Point others toward the One who possesses the world's only light.

To be the city set on a hill means that others are eyeing us. The world is staring at God's people. And that's as it should be. The Lord has appointed us to be *watched*; we've been appointed to *shine*. But if a church extinguishes her message or her good deeds, if the church doesn't lift up Christ, then the world cannot see and will not see the One who is the light of the world.

Our cities need Christ. The church—God's people—bear witness to Christ. As a city within a city, our urban churches must recapture our identity as an alternative, light-giving, glory-inducing community within the larger urban community. This will give the means for God's fame and name to spread through the world's great cities.

A CLOSING PRAYER

Father, we praise you as the One who said, "Let there be light." And we thank you for the One who came into our world to say to us, "I am the light of the world" and "You are the light of the world.

Lord, continue to illumine our hearts and our lives and our eyes through your magnificent and radiant light of splendor. Let us shine in our workplaces and families and neighborhoods, in the midst of this world of darkness.

Do this so that others might see, so those around us might see a city set on a hill.

We pray this in Christ's name,
Amen.

10

GLOBAL CITY GOSPEL MOVEMENTS

The great things of God are beyond our control.
Therein lies a vast hope.

ROLAND ALLEN

The word of God increased and multiplied.

ACTS 12:24

The hope for transformation in our cities *is the church upholding the gospel*. Widespread change, however, will come not merely through changed individuals or even isolated, changed churches; the hope will be realized in *a movement of God*. This is the key to awakening today's urban generation.

Of course, the changing of individuals—what we call discipleship—is indescribably important. So is the planting and establishment and strengthening of churches. As we saw in the last chapter, the church is God's light in every generation. But historically, God often brings a deeper and more radical following of Christ in a widespread way through something we can call *movements*. They're the times in history when something big is happening, something that *God* is clearly the author of, and they have a profound impact on the growth and strengthening of the church at large.

Historically there have been many such movements. In America's history, two of them in particular—known as the First Great Awakening in the mid-1700s and the Second Great Awakening in the early 1800s—had momentous impact.

In the forefront of the First Great Awakening was Jonathan Edwards, the greatest American theologian. Edwards was strongly movement-minded, as evidenced in his book *A Humble Attempt to Promote Prayer for Revival*. It was a work that came together as he meditated on this particular Old Testament prophecy, one with obvious urban implications:

> Thus saith the LORD of hosts; It shall yet come to pass, that there shall come people, and the inhabitants of many cities: And the inhabitants of one city shall go to another, saying, Let us go speedily to pray before the LORD, and to seek the LORD of hosts. (Zech. 8:20–21, KJV)

Notice the urgency here in the people's desire to entreat the Lord, as well as the emphasis on "many cities."

Edwards was convinced that what Zechariah prophesied here had not yet taken place. Edwards foresaw here "that last and greatest enlargement and most glorious advancement of the church of God on earth"; it would be "a prevailing, spreading thing," and it would be marked especially by unified pleading before God: "a visible union in extraordinary, speedy, fervent, and constant prayer."[1]

What would it take to see this in our cities at the dawn of the urban generation?

ANOTHER GREAT AWAKENING

In recent decades, a global church planting movement has intensified, with countless new churches established in cities worldwide. As applied to a particular urban region, this movement has been defined as "a Spirit-directed activity which naturally builds, renews, and expands the body of Christ in a given city/region through the recovery and application of the Gospel."[2]

Here's a listing of what such a movement has been observed to bring about:

- A dramatic increase in the number of disciples (conversions).
- A prevailing deepening of spiritual devotion.
- A widespread increase in evangelistic and social involvement on the part of Christians.
- A noted increase in the church's influence in society.
- Significant multiplication of churches (churches or individuals starting new churches).

- Marked growth in the vitality and maturity of churches.
- Emergence of competent, biblical leadership.[3]

That's the kind of broad impact that's possible only through a movement of God. It represents a relentless advancement and a soul-stirring cause that every believer in the urban generation can become a part of.

To witness the rise of yet another great awakening—to see a vast turning to God in our cities—our urban generation must begin looking beyond the four walls of a local congregation and hunger to participate in God's larger work. This requires a shift in mind-set; it means expanding our focus from the individual to the global, and from the human to the divine; it means recognizing profoundly that God loves your neighbor *and* the world.

A MIGHTY RUSHING WIND

Let's go back to the very first and foremost post-resurrection movement of God in Christian history—the one recorded in the book of Acts. The clear emphasis in this part of Scripture is that here was *God's* work—something beyond human capacity to generate or sustain.

That dynamic is nicely portrayed in the simple phrase "a mighty rushing wind" in Acts 2:2. Such a wind blew in the first instance of what the missions specialist Roland Allen called the church's "spontaneous expansion"—something meant to occur again and again, by God's grace. It can happen in our day, too; and it's well worth our prayers—for it's ultimately beyond our own ability and influence:

> By spontaneous expansion I mean something which we cannot control. . . . Spontaneous expansion could fill the continents with the knowledge of Christ: our control cannot reach as far as that.[4]

But of course, God's control *does* reach that far, and infinitely farther. So will he be at work in our day to fill the cities and the continents with a great turning to the Lord?

Allen, who was British, worked as a missionary in China in the late nineteenth and early twentieth centuries. He critiqued the mission organizations of his day as being shy of God's movement. "Missionaries pray for the wind of the Spirit," he observed, "but not for a rushing mighty wind. I am writing because I believe in a rushing mighty wind, and desire its presence at all costs."[5] He recognized a reason for resistance to this concept: "There is something terrifying in the feeling that we are letting loose a force which we cannot control; and when we think of spontaneous expansion in this way, instinctively we begin to be afraid." But Allen insisted, "Spontaneous expansion must be free; it cannot be under our control."[6]

We can find a number of essential concepts and principles in Acts that show us God's heart for such a "spontaneous" movement. Let's focus in particular on Acts 13, where an exciting new chapter in the church's expansion was being launched during what John Piper has called "the prayer meeting that changed the world."[7] We can observe six key principles here for gospel movements in today's urban regions.

THE PRINCIPLE OF WORSHIP

We find the movement here beginning not with a meeting on mission strategy, but with *worship*:

> Now there were in the church at Antioch prophets and teachers, Barnabas, Simeon who was called Niger, Lucius of Cyrene, Manaen a lifelong friend of Herod the tetrarch, and Saul. *While they were worshiping the Lord and fasting, the Holy Spirit said,* "Set apart for me Barnabas and Saul for the work to which I have called them." Then after fasting and praying they laid their hands on them and sent them off. (Acts 13:1–3)

These men were like sailors at night, looking upward to survey the stars and suddenly finding new direction. They were seeking the glory of God not just in their public ministry as teachers, but also in their fasting and prayers. In the midst of their faithful service, God met them—and God moved them.

The church at Antioch was a praying, worshiping body, and the leaders were in fact praying leaders. This pulsing context of prayer and worship formed a heated core for the incredible explosion of energy we see in the middle and later chapters of Acts, as the gospel rapidly spreads.

THE PRINCIPLE OF THE SPIRIT

Notice here too that from the very beginning, the Holy Spirit was in charge of the mission; it was the Spirit who spoke the divine directive for setting apart Barnabas and Paul—here called Saul.

This is further confirmed a few verses later, where we read that these men were "being sent out by the Holy Spirit" (Acts 13:4). Just a few verses on it's confirmed yet again, as Paul is described as being "filled with the Holy Spirit" (13:9). The Spirit's careful guidance of Paul—in quite surprising ways at times—emerges in later verses as well (16:6–7; 19:21; 20:22–23; 21:4,11).

We don't know precisely *how* God spoke through the Spirit to Paul and his companions—whether his voice was audible or he led through their circumstances, careful planning, or subjective impressions. What we do know is that the Spirit was in charge. He *led*.

It is worth asking: Who's in charge for us? Don't we want the same Spirit-directedness? We do, of course; the awakening movement for the urban generation must be Spirit-guided. The Holy Spirit, active and moving, is the church's only qualified *mobilizer* and *equipper*—as we see also in such passages as 1 Corinthians 12:12–31 and Ephesians 4:1–16.

THE PRINCIPLE OF THE WORD

This emphasis on the Spirit doesn't mean a neglect of the Bible. What often happens in our arrogant dichotomizing is that renewal movements tend to emphasize *either* Word or Spirit. This is a false distinction. Word and Spirit go together in the same way that human speech and breath go together; as we speak, we must have breath.

Acts 13 again bears this out. We see it first in the fact that the five leaders mentioned in the chapter's opening verse were all *proclaimers*. They were preachers. These men loved Jesus and his authority, his ministry, his power, and his work. They proclaimed *him*.

We see it also as the launch is further described for the mission assigned to Paul and Barnabas:

> So, being sent out by the Holy Spirit, they went down to Seleucia, and from there they sailed to Cyprus. When they arrived at Salamis, *they proclaimed the word of God* in the synagogues of the Jews. (Acts 13:4–5)

In this beginning city-to-city movement of the gospel, Spirit and Word were not two separate entities or emphases but went forth hand in hand. The Word was like a sword, and the Spirit the clenched hand that wielded it, as the gospel was preached in life-saving power.

One way to trace this is to follow this theme of the *word* right through all of Acts:

> So those who received his *word* were baptized, and there were added that day about three thousand souls. (Acts 2:41)

> But many of those who had heard the *word* believed, and the number of the men came to about five thousand. (4:4)

> Now those who were scattered went about preaching the *word*. (8:4)

> But the *word of God* increased and multiplied. (12:24)

> And the *word of the Lord* was spreading throughout the whole region. (13:49)

> So they remained for a long time, speaking boldly for the Lord, who bore witness to the *word of his grace*. (14:3)

> And he stayed a year and six months, teaching the *word of God* among them. (18:11)

> This continued for two years, so that all the residents of Asia heard the *word of the Lord*, both Jews and Greeks. (19:10)

> So the *word of the Lord* continued to increase and prevail mightily. (19:20)

Or for added perspective, trace the concept of *gospel proclamation* in Acts, including passages like these:

> And he commanded us to *preach* to the people and to *testify* that he is the one appointed by God to be judge of the living and the dead. To him all the prophets bear witness that everyone who believes in him receives forgiveness of sins through his name. (Acts 10:42–43)

And we bring you the *good news* that what God promised to the fathers, this he has fulfilled to us their children by raising Jesus. (13:32–33)

Let it be known to you therefore, brothers, that through this man forgiveness of sins is *proclaimed* to you. (13:38)

And there they continued to *preach the gospel.* (14:7)

When they had *preached the gospel* to that city and had made many disciples, they returned . . . to Antioch. (14:21)

Finally, in the concluding verse of Acts, we see Paul imprisoned in Rome, yet still "*proclaiming the kingdom of God* and *teaching about the Lord Jesus Christ*" (Acts 28:31).

I hope the pattern emerging in Acts is apparent. We see a movement that 1) began in *service* and *worship*, 2) was directed by the *Holy Spirit*, 3) and then moved forward in *preaching the word* of the good news of Jesus Christ. That's how the first church planting movement began.

Three more principles fill out the picture even more fully.

THE PRINCIPLE OF COMMUNITY

In this movement, God used the apostles to *make disciples.* The result of the worship-fueled, Spirit-directed, preaching-oriented mission is *new disciples*—rejoicing in the word of the Lord—who then gathered into *local communities of the gospel.*

That's the direct outcome we see multiple times in Acts. In chapter 13, we observe it most significantly among the Gentiles in the city of Antioch in Pisidia: "they began rejoicing and glorifying the word of the Lord, and as many as were appointed to eternal life believed" (Acts 13:48). This had come about after Paul met heated resistance to the gospel among the Jews; he then turned instead to the Gentiles, explaining it this way: "For so the Lord has commanded us, saying, 'I have made you a light for the Gentiles, that you may bring salvation to the ends of the earth'" (v. 47).

Then comes more evidence that this was a bona fide *movement*: "And the word of the Lord was *spreading throughout the whole region*" (Acts 13:49). The chapter ends with more indication of spiritual fruit: "And the disciples were filled with joy and with the Holy Spirit" (v. 52).

These disciples were not just isolated individuals journaling every morning at their local Starbucks over a cinnamon scone—that being the substance of their spiritual life. No, these were *churches*, gatherings of the gospel, fellowships of believers.

We know this fact from what we see in the next chapter. Paul, after having proclaimed the gospel in other cities, now backtracked through the region and "appointed elders for them in every *church*," while he also "committed them to the Lord in whom they had believed" (Acts 14:23). Again in 15:41, we read of Paul returning and "strengthening the *churches*" throughout areas where he previously ministered. It was churches he raised up, not solitary believers.

THE PRINCIPLE OF LEADERSHIP

A critical point often overlooked in all this is how the launching of this first missionary movement came through key leadership teams. God often assembles teams of people who together can do more than they could apart from each other.

The Spirit first sent Paul together with Barnabas. Later, when these two separated, they formed two other teams—Barnabas taking John Mark with him, and Paul taking Silas.

By the time we reach Acts 20, the list of Paul's growing team is a long one:

> Sopater the Berean, son of Pyrrhus, accompanied him; and of the Thessalonians, Aristarchus and Secundus; and Gaius of Derbe, and Timothy; and the Asians, Tychicus and Trophimus. (20:4)

These men came originally from areas scattered widely across what is today Greece and Turkey. Paul brought them together as a true ministry team.

Interestingly, the church in Antioch of Syria, the place highlighted in Acts 13 as the birthplace of this movement, was most likely the first multiethnic church. The launching of the global city gospel movement begins in the rich context of multicultural leadership. From the names of the church leaders mentioned in 13:1, it appears that this group included a black African plus others who came originally from widely separated regions throughout the eastern Roman empire.

This principle of diverse leadership is evident also in Paul's selection of Timothy—who was half-Jewish, half-Greek—as his ministry companion in Acts 16:1.

THE PRINCIPLE OF CITY

The final observation to draw here—and certainly a key one for this book—is that this initial movement of the gospel flowed naturally toward *cities*, and then into the regions beyond. Paul's mission was an urban mission.

That's not to say Paul and his companions sat down with a map spread before them and picked out cities to target next. They were clearly led by the Spirit, not by their own strategy. But this Spirit-led mission most often was directed to the center of cities.

Antioch itself, where the movement began, was at that time the third largest metropolis in the Roman empire (behind only Rome itself and Alexandria). And though the names we read in Acts of other locations where Paul ministered can sometimes seem obscure to us today, in the first century they represented concentrated points of population and trade and culture. We see Philippi, for example, described as "a *leading city* of the district of Macedonia" (Acts 16:12); similar phrasing could be applied to most of the places where Paul found himself proclaiming the gospel.

Why cities? Here's one scholar's explanation: "The cities were where power was. They were also the places where change could occur."[8] This same scholar writes:

> The mission of the Pauline circle was conceived from start to finish as an urban movement. . . . Within a decade of the crucifixion of Jesus, the village culture of Palestine had been left behind, and the Greco-Roman city became the dominant environment of the Christian movement.[9]

The sound reasoning behind an urban emphasis in missions continues to apply down through the years. As nineteenth-century evangelist D. L. Moody once remarked, "Water flows downhill, and the highest hills in the country are the cities; if we reach them, we shall shake the nation."[10] Cities are the place where culture is made; from there it relentlessly spreads outward. And culture is important.

Roland Allen wrote that for Paul, cities "were centers from which he could start new work with new power. But they were this not only because they were naturally fitted for this purpose, but because his method of work was so designed that centers of intellectual and commercial activity became centers of Christian activity."[11]

Allen adds this regarding the urban centers in Paul's day:

> They were foremost in every movement of policy or thought. . . . They represented something larger than themselves and they looked out into a wider world than the little provincial town which was wholly absorbed in its own petty interests. . . . Through some of them the commerce of the world passed. They were the great marts where the material and intellectual wealth of the world was exchanged.[12]

The same descriptions apply to cities today. Our urban centers remain places of vast influence and potential and power.

So . . . what will we finally do with that fact?

FOR CHRIST

We've explored throughout this book the need for Christ to be central to our cities today. We've pondered how the greatest need in these times is for the gospel to bring life to our cities. Our most urgent call is for the Christ-centered, life-transforming truth of the gospel to take root and bear fruit in the cities of the world.

It begins—and moves forward—as you and I continue following Christ radically and deeply in the urban generation, bound together with our brothers and sisters in the faith in conveying the gospel into ever deeper penetration throughout our cities.

My city, your city, all cities—*they exist for Christ.* May God, through his Holy Spirit, keep deepening this awareness in our souls. May he equip us to better serve his intentions for these people whom he values so highly, helping each and every urban center to fulfill its rightful purpose, to the glory of God alone.

A CLOSING PRAYER

Our Father in heaven,

We remember how your Son told us, "The harvest is plentiful, but the laborers are few. Therefore pray earnestly to the Lord of the harvest to send out laborers into his harvest." So we do ask that you would move again in our cities with the power of the gospel, using teams of men and women who love you.

In the name of Christ we pray,

Amen.

CONCLUSION

Cities and the Future of the World

Successful cities always have a wealth of human energy
that expresses itself in different ways.

EDWARD GLAESER

May people blossom in the cities
like the grass of the field!

PSALM 72:16

Having come to the end, let's revisit the question posed at the beginning: *Where are we going?* What role will cities play in the reaching of our world for Christ? How deep and radical will our own personal following of Christ be at the rise of the urban generation?

God is calling a new generation of awakened urban Christians. We have an opportunity before us to influence our neighbors, our neighborhoods, our cities—and the world. It's the opportunity Jonathan Edwards saw in Zechariah: "This is what the LORD Almighty says: 'Many peoples and the inhabitants of many cities will yet come, and the inhabitants of one city will go to another and say, "Let us go at once to entreat the LORD and seek the LORD Almighty. I myself am going." And many peoples and powerful nations will come to Jerusalem to seek the LORD Almighty and to entreat him'" (Zech. 8:20–22, NIV).[1]

Though writing from a perspective very different from the gospel, Ed Glaeser is right when he points out, "We must free ourselves from our tendency to see cities as their buildings, and remember that the real city is made of flesh, not concrete."[2] From the perspective of the gospel, this means seeing the infinite worth of those around us—something Jonah had forgotten.

God comforted and reminded the apostle Paul while he was in Corinth, "Do not be afraid, but go on speaking and do not be silent, for I am with you, and no one will attack you to harm you, for *I have many in this city who are my people"* (Acts 18:9–10).

We believe God has many in *your* city and *my* city who are his people—those who will rise up to respond to the cross of Christ with faith. This world is passing away; the gospel is more permanent than the City of Man, and it is this gospel that has priority, first for our hearts and then for our cities.

But my hope is that in the years to come—say, over the next seventy years or so (if Christ has not already returned)—awakened urbanites everywhere will invest in their cities for the long-term good of the gospel. Further, my hope is that we'll see, as Ed Glaeser has optimistically pointed out, that our cities (what Glaeser calls our greatest inventions) can be tools and avenues for the spread of the gospel.

When the first Christians were being opposed in their city by the ruling establishment, they were told, "We strictly charged you not to teach in this name, yet here *you have filled Jerusalem with your teaching"* (Acts 5:28). Our hope is that this might be said of all our cities—big or small, diverse or homogenous. May our cities be filled with the teaching of Christ!

Similarly, we learn in Acts that Paul's ministry there had such an effect "that all the residents of Asia heard the word of the Lord, both Jews and Greeks" (Acts 19:10).

For our cities to be filled with the teachings of Jesus, and for the word of the Lord to spread throughout all the surrounding regions, will require that our cities—our greatest invention—become tools of the gospel. Let me close with four final principles for seeing our cities have that kind of impact for the global church in reaching our world.

I look again to the book of Acts in drawing these principles as lessons for us—not prescriptive as things we *must* do, but as observations on the gospel which are instructive. If we want to see today's cities playing an active part in reaching our world for Christ, we'll need a particularly robust gospel Christianity in urban centers—which is exactly what we find in Acts, through the people of the Way (Acts 9:2; 19:9, 23; 24:14, 22).

THE RADIATING GOSPEL

For our cities to be leveraged by the global church to reach our world, they'll first need to be places that emanate the gospel. We touched on this in the last chapter, but it bears emphasis here as we conclude. This "Way" that we read about in Acts radiated from the cities where Paul proclaimed the gospel, continuing to reach outward like ripples from a stone dropped in a pond.

The cities then were more than simply a setting or a backdrop for the gospel. God in fact *used* the city as a *tool* for the transmission of his good news. And he still can. He still does.

Think of the logic behind this. How does the good news circulate? *It spreads by word of mouth.* And since cities are packed with people coming and going—to cities and from cities, to rural and suburban areas as well as to other parts of the world—that means they're teeming with potential communicators of the gospel.

Globalization experts speak of the flows and liquidity of a city. Wayne Meeks, in *The First Urban Christians*, says of the city, "It was the place where, if anywhere, change could be met and even sought out. It was the place where the empire was, and where the future began." He describes not just the ". . . movement of the farmer from his hamlet to the next or to the city to buy and sell or complain to the governor and then back again—but the tides of migration, the risky travel of the merchant, even the irregular movement of manners, attitudes and status."[3]

We have a chance, if our cities are filled with the gospel, to radiate to the regions beyond. This is why Luke can say these remarkable words: "all the residents of Asia heard the word of the Lord" (Acts 19:10).

This doesn't denigrate other means of communication today—internet, media, newspapers, books, magazines. But cities are filled with people, and when the gospel is actively changing people's lives and people are mobile, the gospel radiates.

Cities were fluid in Paul's day also. Roland Allen describes how Paul "seized strategic points because he had a strategy." The cities were centers of commerce, culture, and travel, and Paul went to them intentionally so he could transform them into *spiritual* centers—Christ-centered places. As Allen observes of these cities, to Paul, "the foundation of churches in them was part of a campaign. In his hands they became the source of rivers, mints from which the new coin of the Gospel was spread in every direction."[4]

This is what is needed at the dawn of the urban generation. As the light of a world that is half urban begins to awake, we need cities that radiate the gospel of Jesus Christ in their city and then beyond.

A REASONABLE MESSAGE FOR UNREASONABLE TIMES

Second, for our cities to have an impact for the global church in reaching our world, they'll also need to be places adept at *reasoning* the gospel.

Luke uses an interesting word in Acts 19 in describing Paul's ministry. "And he entered the synagogue and for three months spoke boldly, *reasoning* and persuading them about the kingdom of God" (Acts 19:8). The Greek word translated "reasoning" is *dialegomai,* from which we get our English word "dialogue." The root meaning of *dialegomai* is "through words." It involves exchange, conversation, discussion—and even teaching. It's through *words* that Paul is trying to win them to Christ.

The gospel won't radiate without people who are willing to *engage.* People like you and me have to enter the world and worldview of others and listen, discuss, pray, and converse with them.

In Acts, Paul works hard to explain and persuade as he speaks to a variety of audiences—for example, to the urban Jews in Thessalonica:

> Paul went in, as was his custom, and on three Sabbath days he *reasoned* with them from the Scriptures, *explaining* and *proving* that it was necessary for the Christ to suffer and to rise from the dead, and saying, "This Jesus, whom I proclaim to you, is the Christ." (Acts 17:2–3)

And later in Athens, to Jews as well as others:

> So he *reasoned* in the synagogue with the Jews and the devout persons, and in the marketplace every day with those who happened to be there. (17:17)

Then in Corinth, to Jews as well as Greeks:

> And he *reasoned* in the synagogue every Sabbath, and tried to *persuade* Jews and Greeks. (18:4)

Then in Ephesus:

> . . . they came to Ephesus, and . . . he himself went into the synagogue and *reasoned* with the Jews. (18:19)

And again while revisiting Ephesus, as we saw earlier:

> ... he entered the synagogue and for three months *spoke boldly, reasoning and persuading* them about the kingdom of God. (19:8)

Christianity, the Way, is a *word*-centered faith. The gospel is a message of words, which means it requires speaking in order to grow and multiply.

The gospel will not radiate outward from the centers of cities unless people are speaking and communicating it. The gospel isn't transmitted by some silent, passive osmosis; the gospel moves from person to person only through words. And that's what Paul is doing in Acts.

When I look at the people who are coming to faith in our cities, it happens when the gospel crosses a barrier—through the words of others. I think of a businessman who came to Christ this year; it was a simple invitation to a lunchtime study, teaching from God's Word in a relevant way, and suddenly the gospel took root.

Cities are often bastions of cynicism, but the gospel itself remains inherently reasonable and persuasive. When clearly presented and explained, it's always strong and sound, and with the Spirit's power it is more than able to soften and sway urban doubters, disbelievers, and detractors. The word of the gospel is able to redirect hearts and reshape minds.

There are plenty of urbanites today who think Christianity is unreasonable, but most haven't truly understood the gospel. Others have understood only too well—but repudiate it. For the gospel to radiate, we need the exchange of words that comes from entering into each other's worlds, dialoguing about our worldview, and introducing the person of Christ as Lord.

A RESILIENT GOSPEL FOR A CHANGING CULTURE

Third, for our cities to have an impact in reaching our world, our churches will need great flexibility and resilience.

No one says that ministry in our cities is easy. Paul's urban ministry frequently encountered opposition. "But Jews came from Antioch and Iconium, and having persuaded the crowds, they stoned Paul and dragged him out of the city, supposing that he was dead. But when the disciples gathered about him, he rose up and entered the city, and on the next day he went on with Barnabas to Derbe" (Acts 14:19–20). Luke tells us that when Paul returned to Lystra, he was "strengthening the souls of the disciples, encouraging them to continue in the faith, and saying that through many tribulations we must enter the kingdom of God" (v. 22).

There were hardships in Ephesus as well. After Paul spent three months proclaiming Christ in the synagogue there, opposition arose: "some became stubborn and continued in unbelief, speaking evil of the Way before the congregation." At that, Paul "withdrew from them and took the disciples with him, reasoning daily in the hall of Tyrannus" (Acts 19:9).

There's something about city ministry, and about all ministries that radiate the gospel, that requires the kind of resilience and flexibility that Luke writes of here. It probably is a minor point, but talk to church planters and new churches in urban contexts and you'll find a pattern of movement from place to place; of an open door, and then encountering opposition. Urban Christianity must be robust and gospel-centered, but it must also be resilient and flexible.

One of the reasons for the decline of gospel Christianity in major cities is the inability to adapt the gospel in the face of opposition and a changing context. When urban churches are *not* flexible (usually ending up in decline or closing), it's often because we've confused that which is permanent with that which is transient. We hold on to styles and patterns of doing things that once were links to a city's culture but that over time end up becoming barriers as the city's culture inevitably evolves.

One thing that absolutely doesn't change is the person and work of our Savior and Lord, for "Jesus Christ is the same yesterday and today and forever" (Heb. 13:8). To see the awakening of our cities at the dawn of the urban generation, we'll need a movement of Christians who hold to the essence of the unchanging gospel of the unchanging Christ, yet who adapt resiliently in the face of opposition and change.

LEADING TO RIGOROUS DISCIPLESHIP

Finally, for our cities to have an impact for the global church in reaching our world, our churches will need rigorous ministries of discipleship and training. We'll need to train many, many people.

Luke tells us how Paul taught daily in the hall of Tyrannus in Ephesus, and how this "continued for two years." It was during this time that "*all* the residents of Asia heard the word of the Lord" (Acts 19:10). How could Luke say that? This was no small claim. *Asia* at that time referred to a Roman province spreading out from Ephesus, an area about as big as the state of New York or the country of England. To declare that everyone in that large province heard the word of the Lord in those two short years is a staggering statement.

It happened because Paul was committed to training. He believed in the multiplication of ministry in others' lives. That's what the gospel could do when it flowed out in power from a place as influential as Ephesus, after being preached and taught and built into people's lives as was done through Paul's ministry there.

Paul tells Timothy that his ministry should think four generations deep: "What you have heard from me in the presence of many witnesses entrust to faithful men who will be able to teach others also" (2 Tim. 2:2). Those four generations were Paul, Timothy, "faithful men," and "others."

Roland Allen helps us here again: "It is not enough for the church to be established in a place where many are coming and going unless the people who come and go not only learn the Gospel, but learn it in such a way that they can propagate it."[5]

Paul in Ephesus was constantly winning, training and sending people. And as Ephesus saw people constantly coming and going in all directions, this hall of Tyrannus in the city's center became the takeoff point for an unquenchable movement across the entire province and beyond.

This is a model for urban churches today—to become places that are constantly building up disciples and then launching them into other locations and spheres of influence.

That was the vision we had for Holy Trinity in Chicago when we began meeting more than a dozen years ago. Since then, though our church isn't large, we've sent out hundreds of people to other cities like Washington, DC, New York, Boston, Raleigh, London, Seattle, Zurich, and Singapore. There are followers of Jesus all over the world whom the Lord has allowed us for a period of time to train. We've been part of a global movement of God, one that we can still call the Way. It's a movement that involves the radiating of the gospel, the reasonableness of the gospel, and the rigorous discipleship and training that flow from the gospel.

LIVING THE WAY

To bring this down to a more personal level, as you get ready to close this book and continue following Christ in the urban generation, allow me to offer you three charges as a calling on your life. It's a calling for us as awakened urbanites enlivened by the gospel. Our churches in our cities must develop authentic disciples; may you be one of them, following Christ deeply and radically.

1. *Live the Way.* Christianity is about training the mind, but it's about the heart and the head and the hands as well. Part of the reason it's called the Way is that it represents a lifestyle of people sharing fellowship and life together. So I call on you in your city to live the Way, and to call others to this as well.

2. *Trust God's sovereignty in the fluidity of urban life.* Follow the example of Paul, who was absolutely devoted to this message about the Unchanging One, yet was always able to deal flexibly with changing circumstances.

3. *Soak up the Word.* Remember that the gospel is a Word-oriented faith. Soak up the Word in the context of community, as put forth in these words:

> Let us hold fast the confession of our hope without wavering, for he who promised is faithful. And let us consider how to stir up one another to love and good works, not neglecting to meet together, as is the habit of some, but encouraging one another, and all the more as you see the Day drawing near. (Heb. 10:23–25)

As a follower of Jesus, as an awakened urbanite, may you be with people who consciously intend to strengthen you with good news—people who are always thinking, *How can I encourage someone else? How can I strengthen them with the Word?* Weave your lives together in the Word.

THIS IS THE HOUR

Our cities are engines of innovation, and God has used them in the past to bring about great spiritual change. May he do so again today and in the future, through the people who are called the Way, followers of Jesus Christ; through men and women of faith in each city who are absolutely committed to one another and to the Word, that the gospel might radiate through our neighborhoods and cities, to vast regions beyond.

Is it possible that the movement to cities is an open door for the gospel?

Let me close with words from Dick Lucas, a pastor in central London for many years. He gave us the following charge as we launched our first congregation in Chicago:

> We think normally of missionaries as those who are going to far-away places. Yes, that is right. God commands us to go into all the world, but he doesn't tell us how far. Sometimes he commands us to go very close to home. Sometimes very close to home is very pagan.
>
> It is probably true to say that missionary work [in urban contexts] will be far harder than among tribes in far-off lands. When you go to a far-off land, you are going to the people who have never heard the gospel and for whom it is genuinely good news for the first time. Here you are going to sophisticated tribes who have heard the truth in generations past, who have turned away from it, who have constructed their own ideologies and idolatries which are tough and seemingly impregnable. . . . *So this is real missionary work, and let's not think that it's less missionary because it's close to home.*

What a great need, and what a great opportunity!

May God raise up a new generation of urban laborers for the church, for his glory!

A CLOSING PRAYER

Father in heaven,

Thank you for the vibrancy of the gospel which has come to us. We ask that you would use us to follow Christ more radically and deeply in this urban generation. Help us to see not just the priority of the gospel, but its permanence—that its effect will outlive our cities. Give our churches the highly virulent community called the Way, the community that is Spirit-empowered and Christ-centered and kingdom-anticipating.

Work in us, so that together we can be flexible, dynamic, fluid, and responsive, seizing the opportunities you provide.

May your gospel continue to grow in our hearts.

We pray this in the name of Jesus Christ and for his sake and glory, Amen.

ACKNOWLEDGMENTS

I have *many* people to thank who have encouraged me along the way:

The thirty-seven adults who had the faith to join the initial core group of HTC almost fifteen years ago.

Elders, deacons, community group leaders, members of HTC: thank you for your love and faith, for wanting to join in following Christ in this urban adventure, and for giving birth to HTC Hyde Park, Downtown, West, and North.

Dave and Lisa Helm: thanks for the green napkin moment in 1996 and ten thousand others since then. I thank God for your friendship and faithfulness in ministry.

My colleagues at HTC—our Antioch team—David, Arthur, Oscar, Joseph, and Tom: thank you for your friendship and the joy of doing ministry together.

Catherine Anderson, who led Hope for Chicago with joy and diligence: thanks for teaching and inspiring us to love the least in our city.

Joseph, Rod, Jackson, Hutz, Mark, and the men at the Chicago Partnership for Church Planting: thanks for your friendship, vision, and desire to see our city filled with new churches.

My mentors Kent and Barbara Hughes: thank you for your friendship over the last twenty-three years, your model of faithfulness in ministry, your love for God's Word, and teaching us when to jump off the pier.

I'm thankful to Dick Lucas, who has trained so many to preach and who reminded us at the beginning, "When God opens doors, no one can shut them."

I want to thank Tim Keller, whom I met first in London in 2000, and whose love for the city has shaped my own. My thanks also to his team at Redeemer City to City, who have helped and encouraged me, especially Mark Reynolds and Al Barth.

John Leonard at Westminster Theological Seminary: my thanks for your excitement for this project.

The pastors who have influenced me along the way.

John Piper, my pastor in college: I'm grateful for your love for the sovereignty of God and glory of Christ.

Sam, Bryan, Eddie, and Joseph, and the team who designed our 2012 Christ + City event.

Thomas Womack, my editor, who encouraged me in this project and helped to give shape to this book.

Crossway's team: I'm thankful for your vision and enthusiasm for publishing quality gospel-centered material; thank you, Justin and Al, for taking on this project and so many others.

Darrin Patrick: thanks for inviting me into your city-to-city cohort and introducing me to great men who love the city but love Jesus more.

Steve and Carol, you are a daily—sometimes hourly—encouragement to press on in the gospel; Phil and Lisa, we're grateful for your friendship and your love for Christ, city, and kingdom; Paul, thanks for keeping everything running and keeping us all sane.

My parents: thanks for taking me to live in my first city, Chicago, at age three, and the second, Zurich, at age five; but thank you mostly for showing me the way to Jesus.

My enormous and wonderful family—Geoff, Jenay, Sasha, Rachel, Josh, Noah, Jessica; your spouses and children are amazing!

I want to thank especially my wife, Amy, for twenty-five years of marriage, for paying for so many of those early dates in college, and being willing to move with me.

And to my children, Micah, Julia, Liza, Anna, and Josh: you are "my joy and crown"; "I thank my God . . . in every prayer of mine for you" (Phil. 4:1; 1:3–4). Thank you for learning to love the city, for countless dinner table conversations, and for listening when I opened the Bible (again).

And to my King and Savior Jesus Christ, I thank you for your sacrifice for me; I look forward to the Eternal City together.

NOTES

INTRODUCTION

1. Ralph Waldo Emerson, *The Selected Letters of Ralph Waldo Emerson*, ed. Joel Myerson (New York: Columbia University Press, 1997), 208.
2. Jean-Jacques Rousseau, *Emile: or On Education*, trans. Alan Bloom (New York: Basic Books, 1979), 59.
3. Albert Camus, *The Fall*, and *Exile and the Kingdom*, trans. Justin O'Brien (New York: Modern Library, 1964), 118.
4. Edward Glaeser, *Triumph of the City: How Our Greatest Invention Makes Us Richer, Smarter, Greener, Healthier, and Happier* (New York: Penguin, 2011); Richard Florida, *The Rise of the Creative Class: And How It's Transforming Work, Leisure, and Everyday Life* (New York: Basic Books, 2002); Saskia Sassen, *The Global City* (Princeton, NJ: Princeton University Press, 2001).

1. WHERE ARE WE GOING?

1. Mike Davis, on the opening page of his 2007 book *Planet of Slums*, movingly described this momentous yet "entirely unnoticed" occasion when "for the first time the urban population of the earth will outnumber the rural" (Mike Davis, *Planet of Slums* [New York: Verso, 2006], 1).
2. See *World Urbanization Prospects, The 2011 Revision: Highlights* from the United Nations Department of Economic and Social Affairs, revised March 2012; accessed June 30, 2012, at http://esa.un.org /unpd/wup/pdf/WUP2011_Highlights.pdf.
3. Parag Khanna, "Beyond City Limits," *Foreign Policy* (September/October 2010), accessed April 20, 2012 at http://www.foreignpolicy .com/articles/2010/08/16/beyond_city_limits?page=full.
4. Khanna, "Beyond City Limits," 126; idem, *How to Run the World* (New York: Random House, 2011).
5. Davis, *Planet of Slums*, 19.
6. Ibid., 205.

7. Glaeser, *Triumph of the City*. Quotations from Glaeser in this chapter are from the book's introduction, pages 1–16.

8. Augustine, in *Saint Augustine: The City of God*, trans. Marcus Dods (New York: Modern Library, 1950), 346.

9. From Thomas Merton's introduction in Augustine, *Saint Augustine: The City of God*, xvii.

10. Augustine, in *Saint Augustine: The City of God*, 866.

11. Nicholas D. Kristof and Sheryl WuDunn, *Half the Sky: Turning Oppression into Opportunity for Women Worldwide* (New York: Vintage, 2009); Rath's story is told in the introduction, xi–xxii.

12. Kristof and WuDunn, *Half the Sky*, xvii.

13. See also Matthew 5:22,29–30; 10:28; 11:23; 16:18; 18:9; 23:15, 33; Mark 9:43–47; Luke 10:15; 12:5; 16:23; Acts 2:27,31; James 3:6; 2 Peter 2:4; Revelation 1:18; 6:8; 20:13–14.

14. Raymond J. Bakke, *Urban Mission: God's Concern for the City*, ed. John E. Kyle (Downers Grove, IL: InterVarsity, 1988), 72.

2. AMBITION AND THE FIRST CITY

1. *Fast Company* magazine, May 2008, as quoted in "The Chicago Spire" at the Chicago Architecture Info website, http://www.chicago architecture.info/ShowBuilding/357.php; accessed April 30, 2012.

2. As reported by David Galbraith on the website "Oobject: A Curations Creation," accessed July 21, 2012, at http://www.oobject.com /category/15-skyscrapers-on-hold.

3. Richard Florida, *The Rise of the Creative Class: And How It's Transforming Work, Leisure, and Everyday Life* (New York: Basic Books, 2002); idem, *Cities and the Creative Class* (London: Routledge, 2004).

4. Florida, *Rise of the Creative Class*, 5.

5. Carl Swanson, "105 Minutes with Boris Johnson," *New York* (June 25, 2012); accessed July 22, 2012, at http://nymag.com/news /intelligencer/encounter/boris-johnson-2012-6/index1.html.

6. See Nahum Sarna, *Genesis*, JPS Torah Commentary (Philadelphia: Jewish Publication Society, 2001), 82. Sarna writes of the ziggurat, "Rooted in the earth, with its head lost in the clouds, it was taken to be the meeting point of heaven and earth, and, as such, the natural arena of divine activity."

7. See Gordon J. Wenham, *Genesis 1–15*, Word Biblical Commentary (Dallas: Word, 1987), 240.

8. John Calvin, *Genesis*, Crossway Classic Commentaries (Wheaton, IL: Crossway, 2001), 103.

9. Calvin, *Genesis*, 104.

10. As reported in *The Wall Street Journal Online*, May 8, 2012; accessed on that date at http://online.wsj.com/article/SB100014240527023 04451104577390392329291890.html?mod=djemTAR_t.

11. See Wenham, *Genesis 1–15*, 240.

12. Calvin, *Genesis*, 105.

13. Ibid. (at Gen. 11:6).

14. Bruce K. Waltke with Cathi J. Fredricks, *Genesis: A Commentary* (Grand Rapids, MI: Zondervan, 2001), 183.

15. Ibid.

16. Augustine, in *Saint Augustine: The City of God*, trans. Marcus Dods (New York: Modern Library, 1950), 477.

17. William Edgar, "Augustine's *City of God*: Two Cities, Two Loves," in *A Faith and Culture Devotional: Daily Readings on Art, Culture, and Life*, ed. Kelly Monroe Kullberg and Lael Arrington (Grand Rapids, MI: Zondervan, 2008), 124.

3. PRAYER AND THE CITY

1. Eric Metaxas, *Socrates in the City: Conversations on "Life, God, and Other Small Topics"* (New York: Dutton, 2011), 81.

2. Leif Enger, *Peace Like a River* (New York: Grove, 2001), 248.

3. Paul E. Miller, *A Praying Life: Connecting with God in a Distracting World* (Colorado Springs: NavPress, 2009), 65.

4. Ibid., 39.

5. Ibid., 41.

6. Ibid.

7. Samuel Irenaeus Prime, *The Power of Prayer Illustrated in the Wonderful Displays of Divine Grace at the Fulton Street and Other Meetings in New York and Elsewhere, in 1857 and 1858* (New York: Scribner, 1859), 21. All details of Lanphier's story in this chapter are taken from Prime's account.

8. Prime, *Power of Prayer*, 27.

9. Ibid., 47.
10. Ibid., 37.
11. Ibid., v.
12. Jonathan Edwards, *An Humble Attempt to Promote Explicit Agreement and Visible Union of God's People in Extraordinary Prayer, for the Revival of Religion and the Advancement of Christ's Kingdom on Earth* (Boston, 1748).
13. Dietrich Bonhoeffer, *Life Together* (New York: Harper & Row, 1954), 29.
14. D. Martyn Lloyd-Jones, *Preaching and Preachers* (Grand Rapids, MI: Zondervan, 1972), 170.
15. Annie Dillard, *Holy the Firm* (New York: Harper & Row, 1977), 59.
16. Some may feel we're imposing our own framework here. But this is how wisdom literature (Psalms, Proverbs, etc.) is intended to be read.
17. Leland Ryken, *Words of Delight: A Literary Introduction to the Bible* (Grand Rapids, MI: Baker, 1992), 230.

4. THE CITY TRANSFORMED

1. As quoted in "Road Rage: Where Your City Ranks," at the WebMD website, accessed May 15, 2012, at http://www.webmd.com/balance/stress-management/news/20090617/road-rage-where-your-city-ranks.
2. Joyce Baldwin, "Jonah," in *The Minor Prophets: An Exegetical and Expository Commentary,* ed. Thomas Edward McComiskey (Grand Rapids, MI: Baker, 2009), 582.
3. Four times in Jonah, God calls Nineveh "great" (1:2; 3:2, 3; 4:11). Interestingly, in Jonah 4:1 the greatness of Jonah's displeasure is specifically contrasted with Nineveh's greatness. The same Hebrew term, *gâdôl,* is translated "exceedingly" in regard to Jonah's displeasure and "great" in regard to Nineveh.
4. Dale M. Brown, *Mesopotamia: The Mighty Kings* (New York: Time-Life, 1995), 17.
5. Ibid., 24.
6. A. K. Grayson, *Assyrian Royal Inscriptions,* 2 vols. (Wiesbaden, Germany: Otto Harrassowitz, 1976), 2:124–125; as quoted by Alfonso

Archi, "Two Heads for the King of Ebla," in *Boundaries of the Ancient Near Eastern World,* ed. Meir Lubetski, Claire Gottlieb, and Sharon Keller (Sheffield, England: Sheffield Academic Press, 1998), 386.

7. Janet Howe Gaines, *Forgiveness in a Wounded World: Jonah's Dilemma* (Atlanta: Society of Biblical Literature, 2003), 82.

8. Ibid., 82–83.

5. FAITHFULNESS IN THE CITY

1. From back-cover endorsements by William Cronon and Ann Durkin Keating for Carl Smith's *The Plan of Chicago: Daniel Burnham and the Remaking of the American City* (Chicago: University of Chicago Press, 2006).

2. From the cover description of the 1993 Princeton Architectural Press edition of Burnham and Bennett's *Plan of Chicago.*

3. Daniel H. Burnham and Edward H. Bennett, *The Plan of Chicago* (Chicago: The Commercial Club, 1909), 1.

4. Charles Moore, *Daniel H. Burnham: Architect, Planner of Cities,* 2 vols. (New York: Houghton Mifflin, 1921), 2:147.

5. Smith, *Plan of Chicago,* 157.

6. C. S. Lewis, *Surprised by Joy: The Shape of My Early Life* (New York: Harcourt, Brace, Jovanovich, 1955), 68.

7. Quoted in Richard J. Mouw, *Uncommon Decency: Christian Civility in an Uncivil World* (Downers Grove, IL: InterVarsity Press, 1992), 147.

8. You can read about how God radically changed John Perkins's life in his book *Let Justice Roll Down* (Ventura, CA: Gospel Light, 1976). Perkins writes that his assailants were "like savages—like some horror out of the night. And I can't forget their faces, so twisted with hate. It was like looking at white-faced demons. Hate did that to them. But you know, I couldn't hate back. When I saw what hate had done to them, I couldn't hate back" (158).

9. Moore, *Daniel H. Burnham,* 12.

10. As quoted by Moore in *Daniel H. Burnham,* 147. Writing in 1921, Moore described this quotation as Burnham's "oft-repeated injunction, formulated in 1907, which has become the motto of city-planners since that day."

6. SEX AND THE CITY

1. Dennis F. Kinlaw, "Song of Songs," in *Psalms, Proverbs, Ecclesiastes, Song of Songs*, vol. 5 of The Expositor's Bible Commentary, ed. Frank E. Gaebelein (Grand Rapids, MI: Zondervan, 1990), 1210.

2. Tom Gledhill, *The Message of the Song of Songs*, The Bible Speaks Today series (Downers Grove, IL: InterVarsity, 1994), 27.

3. *New Geneva Study Bible* (Nashville: Thomas Nelson, 1995), introduction to Song of Solomon, "Characteristics and Themes."

4. Quoted in R. E. Murphy, *The Song of Songs*, Hermeneia Commentaries (Minneapolis: Fortress, 1990), 6; as cited in Tremper Longman III, *Song of Songs*, New International Commentary on the Old Testament (Grand Rapids, MI: Eerdmans, 2001), 21.

5. Gledhill, *Message of the Song of Songs*, 21, 23.

6. The identity of the speakers is inferred from Hebrew through identification of "possessive pronoun endings and verbal forms . . . identified as masculine or feminine, singular or plural" (Gledhill, *Message of the Song of Songs*, 38). This inferred identity can still be mistaken. See Longman, *Song of Songs*, 42, 89.

7. I agree with Longman's reading that Song of Songs is a collection of love poems, almost an anthology. See Longman, *Song of Songs*, 43, 88. This reading is less concerned with an overall narrative arc or a story that must be reconstructed.

8. Gledhill, *Message of the Song of Songs*, 20.

9. While it may seem out of place to our modern ears, the woman is asserting that love has an arousing power that must be respected.

10. Gledhill, *Message of the Song of Songs*, 177.

11. Wendell Berry, *Sex, Economy, Freedom, and Community: Eight Essays* (New York: Pantheon, 1994), 140.

12. Mike Mason, *The Mystery of Marriage* (Portland, OR: Multnomah, 1985), 71.

13. C. S. Lewis, *Surprised by Joy: The Shape of My Early Life* (New York: Harcourt, Brace, Jovanovich, 1955), 221.

14. C. S. Lewis, "The Weight of Glory," in *The Weight of Glory and Other Addresses* (1949; repr., New York: HarperCollins, 1976), 26.

7. ETHNICITY AND THE CITY

1. Suetonius, *The Lives of the Twelve Caesars*, chapter on Claudius, section 25.
2. As reported by Adam Cohen and Elizabeth Taylor in *An American Pharaoh: Mayor Richard J. Daley: His Battle for Chicago and the Nation* (New York: Little, Brown, 2000), 395–396. See also the sermon by Martin Luther King, Jr., "Remaining Awake through a Great Revolution," in *A Knock at Midnight: Inspiration from the Great Sermons of Martin Luther King, Jr.*, ed. Clayborne Carson and Peter Halloran (New York: Warner, 1998), 217, as quoted by Larry L. McSwain and William Loyd Allen in *Twentieth-Century Shapers of Baptist Social Ethics* (Macon, GA: Mercer University Press, 2008), 193.

8. CHILDREN IN THE CITY

1. Timothy J. Keller, *Center Church: Doing Balanced, Gospel-Centered Ministry in Your City* (Grand Rapids, MI: Zondervan, 2012).
2. This and the additional Kathy Keller quotations in this chapter are from her article "Why the City Is a Wonderful Place to Raise Children," posted February 15, 2012, on The Gospel Coalition blog, accessed June 23, 2012, at http://thegospelcoalition.org/blogs/tgc/2012/02/15/why-the-city-is-a-wonderful-place-to-raise-children/ (emphasis hers).
3. Some important early manuscripts do not actually contain the words "in Ephesus" in Ephesians 1:1. For further discussion, see Peter Thomas O'Brien, *The Letter to the Ephesians*, The Pillar New Testament Commentary (Grand Rapids, MI: Eerdmans, 1999), 84–86; and D. A. Carson, Douglas J. Moo, and Leon Morris, *An Introduction to the New Testament* (Grand Rapids, MI: Zondervan, 1992), 311.
4. From the online article "Temple of Artemis," *Encyclopedia Romana*, accessed June 22, 2012, at http://penelope.uchicago.edu/~grout/encyclopaedia_romana/greece/paganism/artemis.html.
5. See Clinton E. Arnold, *Ephesians, Power and Magic: The Concept of Power in Ephesians in Light of Its Historical Setting* (Cambridge: Cambridge University Press, 1989), 27.
6. O'Brien, *Letter to the Ephesians*, 441.
7. See Paul Vitz, "The Importance of Fatherhood," in Eric Metaxas,

Socrates in the City: Conversations on "Life, God, and Other Small Topics" (New York: Dutton, 2011), 86.

8. See *paideia*, in Walter Bauer et al., *A Greek-English Lexicon of the New Testament and Other Early Christian Literature*, 3rd ed., rev. and ed. Frederick William Danker (Chicago: University of Chicago Press, 1957, 1979, 2000).

9. THE CITY WITHIN A CITY

1. D. Martyn Lloyd-Jones, *Studies in the Sermon on the Mount* (Leicester, England: Inter-Varsity Press, 1959), 159–169.

2. Ibid., 142.

3. Steve Timmis, posted online on Twitter, @STimmis, 28 April 2011; accessed June 20, 2012 at https://twitter.com/STimmis/statuses /63540834687135744. See also Tim Chester and Steve Timmis, *Total Church: A Radical Reshaping around Gospel and Community* (Wheaton, IL: Crossway, 2008).

4. Lloyd-Jones, *Studies in the Sermon on the Mount*, 143.

10. GLOBAL CITY GOSPEL MOVEMENTS

1. Jonathan Edwards, *A Humble Attempt to Promote Prayer for Revival* (1746; reprinted at the Revival Library website, accessed July 10, 2012, at http://www.revival-library.org/catalogues/miscellanies /prayer/edwards.html).

2. Timothy J. Keller and J. Allen Thompson, *The Redeemer Church Planting Manual* (New York: Redeemer Church Planting Center, 2008).

3. J. Allen Thompson, "The Church Multiplication Agenda: Filling the Earth with God's Glory" (unpublished paper, 2001); see http://www .google.com/url?sa=t&rct=j&q=&esrc=s&source=web&cd=1&cad= rja&ved=0CCEQFjAA&url=http%3A%2F%2Fwww.icpctraining.com %2Fmove%2Fmovedocs%2Ffiles%2FReflections%2520on%2520 CP%2520Movements.doc&ei=Zk6TULuRJMSYygGLhIHoCQ&usg= AFQjCNGji5lWZfU_HBtNMwLEXuGzlFk_Og&sig2=hDnRVeCL2kmT RqcWMhGY4A.

4. Roland Allen, *The Spontaneous Expansion of the Church* (orig. ed., London: World Dominion Press, 1927; repr., Eugene, OR: Wipf & Stock, 1997), 3.

5. Ibid., 7.

6. Ibid., 3.

7. See http://www.desiringgod.org/resource-library/sermons/prayer -fasting-and-the-course-of-history.

8. Wayne A. Meeks, *The First Urban Christians: The Social World of the Apostle Paul* (New Haven, CT: Yale University Press, 2003), 15.

9. Ibid., 10–11.

10. Quoted in Paul Dwight Moody and Arthur Percy Fitt, *The Shorter Life of D. L. Moody*, vol. 1 (Chicago: The Bible Institute Colportage Association, 1900), 79; see also http://books.google.com/books?id=7TI3 AAAAMAAJ&printsec=frontcover#v=onepage&q&f=false.

11. Roland Allen, *Missionary Methods: St. Paul's or Ours?* (Grand Rapids, MI: Eerdmans, 1962), 17.

12. Ibid., 15–16.

CONCLUSION: CITIES AND THE FUTURE OF THE WORLD

1. Edwards cited this passage in, *A Humble Attempt to Promote Prayer for Revival* (1746; reprinted at the Revival Library website, accessed July 10, 2012, at http://www.revival-library.org/catalogues/miscellanies /prayer/edwards.html).

2. Edward Glaeser, *Triumph of the City: How Our Greatest Invention Makes Us Richer, Smarter, Greener, Healthier, and Happier* (New York: Penguin, 2011), 15.

3. Wayne Meeks, *The First Urban Christians* (New Haven, CT: Yale University Press: 1983), 16.

4. Roland Allen, *Missionary Methods: St. Paul's or Ours?* (Grand Rapids, MI: Eerdmans, 1962), 17.

5. Ibid., 13.

GENERAL INDEX

Abel, 37
Abram/Abraham, 38, 40, 47, 48, 55, 64, 133; faith of, 44–45; as a model for prayer, 56
Alexandria, 169
Allen, Irving Lewis, 147
Allen, Ronald, 161, 163–164, 170, 175
Andrew, 151
anger, 65–66; of Jonah, 72–73
Antioch, 164, 167, 168, 169
Aristarchus, 168
Artemis (Diana), temple of, 134–135
Asaph, generational perspective of, 85–86
Assyria, 25, 67, 68
Athens, 176
Augustine, 23, 28, 45–46

Babel. See Tower of Babel
Babylon, 38, 43, 81, 88; God's plan for, 84–85; God's promise concerning, 90; Jewish exiles in, 82–83, 91–92, 93
Barnabas, 164, 165, 168
Bennett, Edward H., 79–80
Berry, Wendell, 108–109
Bonhoeffer, Dietrich, 59
Burnham, Daniel H., 79–80, 88, 189n10

Cain, 37
Calvin, John, 39, 42
Camus, Albert, 15
case histories: Ming-Un, 157; Rebekah, 19–20
Center Church: Doing Balanced, Gospel-Centered Ministry in your City (T. Keller), 131

Central Park, influence of on Manhattan, 85
Chicago, 36, 89, 121. See also Chicago Spire; Plan of Chicago
Chicago Spire, 35–36, 37
children, raising of in the city, 131–133; and the American dream, 142–143; and the delicacy of children, 141; and the fabric of raising children, 137–138; and God's promise to "live long in the land," 138–140; and God's vision for thriving homes, 133–135; and parenting as a school of discipleship, 141–143; and Paul's Christ-centered vision for raising children, 135–137; and Paul's warning to fathers, 140–141
Christian Community Development Association, 86
Christianity, 112, 115, 138, 174, 180; decline of in major cities, 178; and the training of the mind, 180; urban Christianity, 12, 178; as a word-centered faith, 177
Christians, 15, 27–28, 45, 93, 128, 150, 153, 174, 178; first-century Christians, 23; murder of, 123; in Rome, 93; urban Christians, 12, 13, 173
church planting: contemporary global church planting movement, 162–163; God's post-resurrection work in the "spontaneous expansion" of the church, 163–164
cities, 11, 76, 180–181; as the "abyss of the human species," 14; Christ as central to, 23, 170; developing plans for, 92–94;

SCRIPTURE INDEX

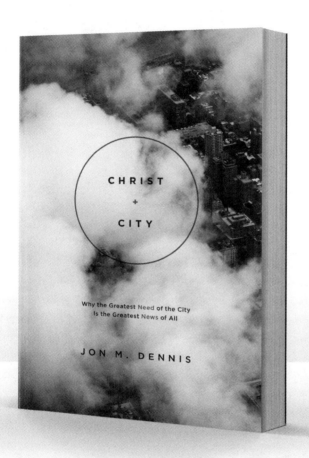

CHRIST
+
CITY

Why the Greatest Need of the City
Is the Greatest News of All

JON M. DENNIS

Christ + City exists to see the supremacy of Jesus
Christ radiate to the great cities of the world.
For more information, go to Christandcity.com.